M000227712

Slang U.

Slang U.

by

Pamela Munro

with

Susan E. Becker, Gina Laura Bozajian,
Deborah S. Creighton, Lori E. Dennis,
Lisa Renée Ellzey, Michelle L. Futterman,
Ari B. Goldstein, Sharon M. Kaye,
Elaine Kealer, Irene Susanne Veli Lehman,
Lauren Mendelsohn, Joseph M. Mendoza,
Lorna Profant, and Katherine A. Sarafian

Harmony Books/New York

—For Alex, who will never use a slang word—

Copyright © 1989 by Pamela Munro

All rights reserved. No part of this book may be reproduced or transmitted in any form or by any means, electronic or mechanical, including photocopying, recording, or by any information storage and retrieval system, without permission in writing from the publisher.

Published by Harmony Books
Member of the Crown Publishing Group.

201 East 50th Street,
New York, New York 10022.

HARMONY and colophon are trademarks of Crown Publishers, Inc.
Manufactured in the United States of America
Library of Congress Cataloging-in-Publication Data

Munro, Pamela.
Slang U. / Pamela Munro.—1st ed.
p. cm.
Includes bibliographical references (p.   ) and index.
1. College students—United States—Language (New words, slang, etc.)—Dictionaries.
2. English language—United States—Slang—Dictionaries.
I. Title.
PE3727.S8M86 1991

427'.09'03—dc20

90-5142
CIP

ISBN 0-517-58243-0   10 9 8 7 6 5 4 3 2 1   First Harmony Books Edition

Contents

—

Acknowledgments

—

➤ We are grateful to two chairmen of the UCLA Linguistics Department, Professors Paul Schachter and Russell Schuh, for their support and encouragement of this project. We also gratefully acknowledge the contribution of the five members of the slang seminar who helped begin this Dictionary but did not participate in editing and expanding it for publication, Florencia Aranovich, Diana Geraci, Albert Nicholson, Kelley Poleynard, and Lisa Vanderburg; Victoria Gamboa also contributed to some of the early discussions of this material. Finally, our thanks go to Outi Bat-El, Susan Curtiss, Tomiko Hayashi, Roderick A. Jacobs, Susan Mordechay, and Mari Sakaguchi for help with etymologies for words borrowed from other languages, and to J. P. Munro, who helped with the final editing.

A Brief Guide to the Dictionary Entries

—

➤ There are two types of entries in our Dictionary, main entries and cross-references.

➤ Main entries have a minimum of two parts and may have a number of others. A main entry begins with a slang word or expression (in **boldface** type), which is followed by its definition. If the entry word has more than one variant form or spelling, the alternative forms are listed together at the beginning of the entry, separated by slashes (/). The part of speech and usage of the definition match those of the entry word. If the word has more than one meaning, these are listed separately, with a different number for each definition. (The order in which different definitions are presented is not significant.) Words that we have judged as being potentially offensive to some people, and which should thus be used with discretion in conversation, are listed in angled brackets (< >). (If every use of an entry is offensive in this sense, the entry itself is enclosed in < >; if only some definitions are offensive in this sense, only those definitions are so marked.) Slang words listed in our Dictionary that are used in definitions appear in *italics*.

➤ In addition to the entry word or expression and its definition, a main entry may include a pronunciation note (in parentheses); one or more example sentences, separated from the definition and from each other by vertical bars (|); and etymological notes, in brackets ([ ]). The etymological notes include information on the source of words formed directly from other words, references to and citations from Chapman's *New Dictionary of American Slang* (1986), preceded by C plus a page number; references to and citations from my previous collections of college slang (Munro, ed., 1990), preceded by U plus a year; and references to other main entries in our collection, preceded by "see also."

➤ All the entries in our Dictionary are listed alphabetically. When closely related words follow each other in the alphabet, these are grouped together, with derivative words listed as subentries under the main entry word. A subentry always consists of at least a slang word or expression plus a definition, and may have all the parts listed above for a main entry.

➤ Cross-references are given for important words in expressions consisting of more than a single word and for alternative versions of main entries. A cross-reference consists of the slang word (or part of it) plus "see" and a reference to the appropriate main entry.

➤ For more information about many of the points above, plus a discussion of the history of our project and the features of college slang, please see the Introduction.

Pronunciation Guide

—

➤ Phonetic transcriptions are given for words in the Dictionary whose pronunciations might not be obvious, along with comparisons with familiar words. The following phonetic symbols are used in our transcriptions:

a	as in **father**	g	as in **get**	ω	as in **put**
æ	as in **bat**	h	as in **hog**	p	as in **put**
ə	as in **sofa**	i	as in **beat**	r	as in **rod**
ʌ	as in **but**	ι	as in **bit**	s	as in **sod**
ay	as in **my**	ǰ	as in **jog**	š	as in **shod**
b	as in **bat**	k	as in **kit**	t	as in **tog**
č	as in **church**	kʸ	as in **cute**	u	as in **boot**
d	as in **dog**	l	as in **log**	w	as in **wit**
e	as in **eight**	m	as in **mat**	y	as in **yip**
ε	as in **bet**	n	as in **nog**	z	as in **zip**
ɝ	as in **Bert**	ŋ	as in **bang**	ž	as in **pleasure**
f	as in **fog**	o	as in **boat**		

Introduction
—

➤ Everyone has an idea what slang is, but any two people's thoughts on this subject are likely to be different, and there has been little scientific study of the topic. This collection of slang from the University of California, Los Angeles, is presented as a contribution to the literature on college slang and American slang in general.

➤ While there are a number of excellent collections of American slang—the best and most comprehensive recent one is Chapman (1986), a revision and extension of Wentworth and Flexner (1975); Partridge (e.g., 1984, one in a series of revised editions), whose name is most prominently associated with collections of slang, gives some attention to American as well as British slang—the topic has received little study by linguists, despite a recent surge of interest in theoretical approaches to the lexicon. The single exception to this generalization is the work of Connie Eble of the University of North Carolina at Chapel Hill, who publishes a new paper on the slang used by U.N.C. students almost every year (see, for example, Eble, 1979, 1980, 1985, and forthcoming), and recently edited *College Slang 101* (1989), a short "textbook" on slang.

The UCLA Slang Project

➤ I had no particular interest in student slang until I met Professor Eble at a linguistics conference in Houston about seven years ago. (Actually, given the prominence of words for drinking and expressions derived from the media in college slang, it may be significant that the site of our meeting was Gilley's, the Houston country-western bar featured in the movie *Urban Cowboy*.) Her description of her collection of slang expressions from students in her English classes intrigued me, and I began collecting slang expressions from students in my upper-division classes in historical linguistics, the study of how language changes over time. My recent students have used slang expressions as a data base for an examination of semantic change, working with a collection (Munro, ed., 1990) that now contains words and expressions suggested by close to two hundred students in six offerings of this course (in 1983, 1984 (two classes), 1987, 1989, and 1990), and presents a fascinating picture of changes in the meaning and use of a specialized vocabulary few older people are aware of (cf. also Eble, 1980).

➤ In the fall of 1988, given the opportunity to teach a special seminar within the UCLA Honors Collegium, I chose to offer a course on slang. The participants in this seminar included the students who are listed as the authors of this Dictionary, an exceptionally dedicated and creative group with whom it has been a special pleasure to collaborate on this project. They worked exceptionally hard outside of class thinking of words and asking their friends about them, and exceptionally hard in class considering words submitted by their classmates and refining the definitions of them.

➤ Class members made an initial short collection of slang expressions, began reading some of the literature on slang (including many works by Professor Eble), and embarked on a number of special projects. As we considered the items on the list, the students (who ranged from freshmen to graduating seniors, most with no previous background in linguistics) grew increasingly careful and critical in their approach to defining and specifying the usage of our entries and in deciding what did and did not belong in our collection. The words on the slang list came from many sources: unprompted recollections, notes class members took on their own and their friends' conversation, and listings prompted either in specific semantic areas or by previous studies, such as my own collection or work by Eble and others. Most expressions in the Dictionary were well-known to all class members, but some proved to be a bit esoteric; there were no class members who knew the meaning of every item that came up during the seminar.

➤ It was clear that a collection like ours was worth sharing with a wider audience, so I asked Professor Paul Schachter, then chairman of the Linguistics Department, if the department would support publication of the completed Dictionary. Professor Schachter (a quick learner) pronounced an early draft **mondo trick** ('very interesting'!) and agreed. (In this Introduction, words from our slang list are written in boldface, while other cited words, both standard and slang, are in italics. All definitions are given in single quotation marks; note, though, that I have shortened some of these from the full definitions given in the Dictionary.)

➤ After the completion of our seminar, fourteen of the nineteen class members—the coauthors of the present volume—continued meeting regularly for three months to edit and extend the slang list, which was duly published as a volume of the UCLA Occasional Papers in Linguistics series (Aranovich et al., 1989). Later, when Kathy Belden of Harmony Books suggested revising the book for publication, most of the same group of students[1] met regularly again in early 1990 to consider additional words and other necessary changes. (We decided to delete specifically UCLA-related entries and examples to produce a more general work.)

➤ The contributions of my student coauthors have been crucial to the success of this project: they helped decide what words should be included in the Dictionary, how they should be defined, and what would be good examples to illustrate their use. The judgments I present here, for instance, concerning the slang status or offensiveness of particular expressions, are theirs, even though I may refer to them for convenience as "ours." Our group discussions, both in the seminar and in later meetings, touched on many of the points I treat in this Introduction, as did many of the students' written assignments for the seminar.[2] For this reason, of course, I cannot discount the input of the five additional members of the original class (Florencia Aranovich, Diana Geraci, Albert Nicholson, Kelley Poleynard, and Lisa Vanderburg), who contributed many of the words on our original list and helped shape our collective ideas about a number of issues.

What Is Slang?

➤ Defining slang, and college slang in particular, is not as easy at it may seem. Initially one may feel that slang is simply "not proper English" or just whatever is not in a standard dictionary. Following a number of authorities (especially Dumas and Lighter, 1978), however, we decided that a number of categories of words that might fit these criteria should not be included on our list: we thus do not consider substandard expressions like *ain't*, regional or "dialect" expressions, and baby talk words like *doggie*, for example, to be slang. The residue of nonstandard language, however, includes not only true slang but also informal or colloquial language—the sort of words and expressions that anyone might use in conversation or a letter, but that would be out of place in a speech or formal essay.

➤ Most authorities conclude that slang is language whose use serves to mark the user as part of a distinct social group, and we have used this criterion in deciding what expressions qualify as college slang. We have usually tried not to include on our list informal or colloquial expressions that would be familiar, in the same form and with the same meaning, to any English speaker, but have included mainly expressions that are characteristic of American college students in general and UCLA students in particular. A few words on our list, however, have almost exactly the same definition with which they would be listed in a standard dictionary: two examples are **inebriated** 'drunk' and **strumpet** 'slut'. Such words are included in our Dictionary as "revivals"— words that we feel are not in common colloquial use among the general population and whose use is characteristic of student vocabulary. Certain other common expressions that might be known to speakers of any age were included because class participants felt their use, too, was especially typical of campus speech. Some of the decisions we have had to make in compiling our list have been delicate and occasionally arbitrary ones.

➤ A category of words that is often confused with slang is jargon: the specialized vocabulary of a particular group. While words which begin as jargon (in California, for instance, surfers' jargon) sometimes may be transferred to the general slang vocabulary of ordinary speakers, we have tried to eliminate true jargon from our Dictionary. (There is a sense, of course, in which many of the words on our list could be considered student jargon, since they refer to test-taking and other activities not usually practiced by the general population!) A few entries on our list might be considered jargon of special subgroups of the student population, such as fraternity or sorority members.

Where Does Slang Come From?

➤ The slang expressions in our list come from a variety of sources. Many are derived directly from the standard vocabulary with little or no change in meaning: they may be revivals of old standard words that are no longer in general use (like **strumpet**, discussed above) or new uses of standard words or earlier slang expressions. For instance, earlier slang **bug** 'to annoy', a transitive verb, has given rise to an intransitive verb meaning 'to be annoying'; standard informal **chow** 'food' becomes a verb 'to eat'; standard **perpetrate** 'to commit (an offense)' can now be used to mean 'to act fraudulently'. (Detransitivization of standard transitive verbs proves to be particularly common in our data base.) Other slang expressions have completely new definitions for standard words, such as **grovel** 'to make out', or **wrap** 'girlfriend'.

➤ Metaphors play a part in the development of slang vocabulary. For instance, many college slang words for 'drunk' derive from standard words meaning 'destroyed' or 'torn': examples include **blasted, blitzed, bombed, ripped, shredded, slaughtered,** and **tattered**—our Index provides many more examples.[3] Traditional sources (such as Partridge, 1933) frequently observe that slang vocabulary is exceptionally "vivid": we interpret this comment to refer simply to the fact that slang often makes use of novel metaphors. **Blow chunks** initially seems like a disturbingly colorful way to say 'to vomit', yet the literal meaning of this expression is almost the same as the colloquial *throw up:* the difference is that because we have heard *throw up* so many times it has lost its power to shock. Many metaphorical expressions in our list are irreverent —for instance, **Einstein** 'pubic hair' is inspired by the great physicist's wild, curly hair. Some slang words are puns—**Babylon,** for instance, is the place where attractive females (**babes**) come from, and thus may be pronounced like "baby lawn" as well as in the expected way.

➤ A number of our words are derived by what Eble (1979) has called "acronymy": we understand this term to mean the use of initials in forming new expressions. A true acronym, of course, is a set of initials pronounced like an ordinary word (like *NATO,* the North Atlantic Treaty Organization). Our Dictionary includes only a few true acronyms, like **SNAG** 'nice guy' (from *sensitive new-age guy*), and some other expressions which are based on partial acronyms, such as **beemer** 'B.M.W. car.' But there are many other acronymic expresssions in the list consisting of initials pronounced separately such as **M.O.S.** 'member of the opposite sex' or **S.O.L.** 'out of luck' (from *shit out of luck*). As the last example indicates, acronymy often is employed euphemistically. While nearly every expression on our list containing **fuck** was marked offensive by class members (as described below), acronymic expressions like **F.O.!** 'Get out of here!' (from *fuck off*) and **C.F.M.** 'sexually suggestive' (from *come fuck me*) were considered generally inoffensive. In our list, we have followed the convention of writing initials pronounced separately with periods (but no spaces) between them: sequences of initials pronounced as complete words are written without periods.[4]

➤ Another common source for slang expressions is clipping, the shortening of standard words. Often this involves simply dropping part (usually the end) of a word: **def** comes from *definite* or *definitely;* **ob** is from *obvious* or *obviously;* **veg** is from *vegetate.* **Dis** 'be mean to' is an unusual case, from which everything has been clipped except the negative prefix *dis-:* it's not even clear what the source of this word is—*disregard? disrespect? disappoint?* Sometimes more than one clipped word may be combined, as in **sped** 'slow, stupid person' (from *special education*). Other items on the list are blends of two separate slang or standard words, like **dimbo** 'dumb bimbo' and **gork** 'loser', an apparent blend of the slang words **geek** and **dork**.

➤ Still other new slang words are formed from both standard and slang words by regular English derivational processes. For instance, **-ette** is suffixed to create feminine forms of **stud** 'person who has done something outstanding; conceited person' and, perhaps more surprisingly, **mazeh** 'gorgeous guy', a word based on a Hebrew expression (and reportedly coined by former Hebrew school students). The adjectival suffix **-y** combines with **suck** 'to be bad' to form **sucky** 'awful'. The negative prefix **un-** plus the familiar slang word **cool** 'very good, excellent' yields **uncool** 'not good, unfair, tactless'. Compounding is also a common source of slang vocabulary, as words like **beauhunk** 'boyfriend', **brainfart** '(exclamation used about a sudden loss of memory or train of thought)', and **studmuffin** 'strong, muscular person; cute person, achiever' illustrate.

➤ Another process that operates in the development of slang vocabulary (and helps it mystify outsiders) is the ironic use of a word to indicate its semantic opposite. The slang use of **bad** to mean 'good' is well-known; our list also includes such examples as **mental giant** 'unintelligent person', **pretty** 'ridiculous', and **Yeah, right!** 'I don't believe you!' Often such new uses originate with heavy sarcastic intonation, but when the new meaning gains acceptance, this special intonation is no longer required. A number of words on our list have two dramatically different meanings, of which the negative one is original: **badass** 'very good' / 'bad', **deadly** 'very good' / 'very bad', **killer** 'fantastic' / 'bad', **wicked** 'excellent' / 'bad'.

➤ As Eble has observed (1985), many student slang expressions derive from current popular culture. Examples in our list include **Sally** 'meticulous person' (from *When Harry Met Sally,* 1989), **Heather** 'superficial girl' (from *Heathers,* 1989), **bushbitch** 'ugly girl' (from *Eddie Murphy Raw,* 1987), **have missile lock** 'to concentrate on or make a target of someone' (from *Top Gun,* 1986), **McFly** 'person with no intelligence' (from George McFly, a character in *Back to the Future,* 1985), and **slip (someone) the hot beef injection** 'to have sex with (someone)' (from *The Breakfast Club,* 1985). Most such expressions come from the media of the middle to late 1980s, but others persist from earlier periods: **bodacious tatas** 'breasts' is from *An Officer and a Gentleman* (1982); **ralph** 'penis' is from Judy Blume's book *Forever* (1975). Expressions relating to old cartoon shows endure especially well: these include **wilma** 'ugly woman' and other expressions based on "The Flintstones," **scoob** 'to eat, have some food (especially snacks)' (from "Scooby Doo"), and **Magoo** 'old man slowly driving a car' (from "Mr. Magoo"). In contrast, class members felt that several expressions I had collected from students in 1983 that referred to the movie *E.T.* (1982) were extremely dated.

➤ Our Dictionary also includes several words that allude not to popular culture but to classical mythology, such as **adonis** 'extremely nice-looking [of a male]; extremely nice-looking young man' and **nectar** 'alcoholic beverage; outstanding'. **Carpe diem!** 'Go for it!' is a mixture of modern and classical: the Latin phrase for 'Seize the day!' was introduced to today's students in the 1989 movie *Dead Poets Society.* Other entries have equally eclectic sources: Einstein's famous equation (which appears on the frieze of a UCLA building) yields **mc²** 'overly studious', for instance; expressions from German, Hawaiian Pidgin, Italian, Japanese, Spanish, and Yiddish inspired other items on the list.

➤ Etymologies (enclosed in brackets) are shown for many words in the Dictionary. Sources for words derived from other words, like the acronyms discussed above, follow the < "from" sign. In some cases, the parts of a source that form the dictionary word are underlined—thus, for example, the source of **sped** is given as "<special education." Sources are also given for words derived from the media or borrowed from other languages. References are provided for words that appear in the earlier UCLA list (Munro, ed., 1990) or in Chapman, as described in the Brief Guide to the

Dictionary Entries section of this book. A simple reference to either of these sources (preceded by U for UCLA or C for Chapman) means that the word appeared there with the same form and meaning; where there are differences, or when Chapman identifies the first period of a word's use, all or part of the citation is quoted. (Chapman uses the abbreviations "fr" for "from" and "esp" for "especially." His book also contains many useful etymological notes that are not repeated in our collection.) When we are not sure of a word's derivation, a question mark (?) appears in the etymology.

➤ Chapman's etymologies reveal that Black English is an extremely important source of slang expressions. This is obvious with expressions like **homeboy,** which are popularly identified with black culture; our citations from Chapman show that many other expressions, such as **boss** 'great', **ripped** 'drunk', and **kick back** 'to relax', also come from Black English. Real or imagined Black English pronunciation is responsible for other items, such as **ho** (from *whore*) and **thang** (from *thing*).

➤ In addition to words like those discussed above, whose etymology is fairly clear, our list also includes some completely new words that do not appear in any form in standard dictionaries or in collections of slang such as Chapman's. Some examples from our list include **foof** 'superficial person', **Yar!** 'Good!', and **zuke** 'to vomit'. (As Maurer and High [1980] observe, such "true neologisms" are the rarest source of new additions to vocabulary.)

The Perseverance of Slang

➤ Slang words come and go. Some slang expressions are no longer recognized by speakers just a few years later, other slang words come to be accepted as standard language, while still others persist as slang for many years. **Mooch,** a familiar word that the students in the slang seminar felt should be included in our corpus, for example, is identified by Chapman (1986: 282) as having originated in sixteenth-century England.

➤ A commonly noted trait of slang is its ephemerality. Eble's forthcoming article studies retention of American college slang terms, comparing them to earlier recordings dating back to the mid-nineteenth century and finding considerable change in slang expressions over time. The students in the slang seminar studied my previous collection of UCLA slang, begun in 1983 (Munro, ed., 1990), and added those expressions that they considered still current to our Dictionary. Many of the words submitted by earlier students, however, were judged too old to include, and some were not recognized at all.

More About Definitions and Dictionary Entries

➤ All items on our list have definitions that match them, as far as possible, in part of speech and usage: nouns are defined with nouns, adjectives are defined with adjectives, transitive verbs are defined with transitive verbs, and so on. Some interjections do not have a definition as such, but receive only a usage note: for instance, **Swoon!** is an '(exclamation used on noticing a new attractive man)'.

➤ Different definitions of the same word are numbered. Each different part of speech is considered a separate definition, as are extremely different meanings within the same part of speech; transitive and intransitive verbs are also differentiated with different definition numbers. The order in which definitions are listed is arbitrary and has nothing to do with their relative acceptability or frequency of use.

➤ Definitions of many words include other synonymous slang items from our list. These are italicized in the definitions.

➤ Variants of the same expression with the same definition are listed together, separated with a slash (/). Again, the order in which different variants are listed is often arbitrary. (When second or subsequent variants would appear in a different point in the alphabet from the first variant, they receive a cross-reference entry, whose definition begins with "see. . . .")

➤ All verbs have a definition beginning with 'to'; thus, 'to vomit' defines a verb, for instance, while the definition 'vomit' refers to the noun (substance). We have specially listed unexpected past or other forms for some verbs. Normally, all verbs can occur in present singular *(-s)*, past *(-ed)*, and progressive *(-ing)* forms; if not, the unacceptable forms are listed in parentheses with an asterisk (*) following the definition.

When an object noun or noun phrase always appears between two words of a multiword verb phrase, we have put **(someone)** at the appropriate position in the entry for that verb phrase: thus, **give (someone) cavities** 'to be nauseatingly sweet to (someone)' always contains an object word or phrase between a form of **give** and **cavities**: *She gives Mark cavities,* et cetera. Verbs whose objects may occur either in this position or after the whole phrase, however, are not listed with **(someone): blow away** 'to amaze, shock' thus may occur with objects in two positions *(She blew Mark away / She blew away Mark).* (For more about this second type of verb phrase, see the section on slang grammar [page 13].)

A number of verb phrases in our Dictionary include possessed objects. We use **one's** before the object word when the possessor is always the same as the verb's subject: thus, with **shake one's skirt** 'to dance', the possessor of **skirt** is the same as the subject of **shake,** and is always specified with a possessive adjective: *I shake my skirt,* et cetera. In contrast, **(someone's)** is used when the possessor of the object noun in the phrase is different from the subject of the verb—so **spin (someone's) wheels** 'to excite' is used in sentences like *You spin my wheels* or *Larry spins Susie's wheels* in which the subject of **spin** and the possessor of **wheels** are different.

➤ Some entries include blanks (___) where a word of the speaker's choice may be inserted. The definitions clarify the type of word that can be used to fill in these blanks.

➤ We have tried to be very strict about the use of nouns with articles in our entries and definitions. Nouns referring to people defined with 'person', for instance, can be preceded by an indefinite article, since *person* can, for example (such as **Cap'n Toke** 'person who smokes marijuana a lot'—thus, one could say *He's a total Cap'n Toke).* On the other hand, nouns for people that are not used with articles are defined with 'someone', which cannot be used with an article (an example is **Tina Tridelt** 'someone female who is incredibly superficial looking or acting, who may or may not be a sorority member'—thus, one might say *She's Tina Tridelt).* Some noun phrases (such as **the shake** 'an undesirable person' or **the crib** 'home') always include the article **the;** we have alphabetized these under **the** (of course, the following word in the expression always receives a cross-reference at its own point in the alphabet).

➤ Pronunciations are listed for some words following their definitions. Most of these are listed in two ways: with a phonetic transcription in brackets ([ ]), and with a comparison to other familiar words. (A list of the phonetic symbols [page xi] used in our transcriptions follows the Brief Guide to the Dictionary Entries.) As noted above, words consisting only of initials pronounced as separate letters are written with periods between the letters.

➤ In college slang the present participial verb ending -**ing** is very often pronounced as -**in**, with a final **n**. Since these final -**in**'s can always be replaced by -**ing**, in a slightly more formal style of speech, we have written all present participles with -**ing** in our list; it should be noted, however, that the -**in** pronunciation may often sound more natural. There are two exceptions to this generalization: **bitchin** 'good, excellent' and **illin**, in **be illin** 'to act stupid'. We have seen these two words written with -*in*', but we cannot easily identify them as present participles of any verb and have only heard them pronounced with **n**; therefore, we do not write them with -**ing**.

The Index

➤ An Index following the main section of the Dictionary lists the entries according to their basic meaning, providing a useful guide to slang synonyms and an indication of the frequency with which various concepts are expressed in college slang. Writing about the first version of the Dictionary, *Los Angeles Times* columnist Jack Smith (1989) observed that it contained "more words for drunkenness, throwing up, and sex"—or, as he later put it, "boozing, barfing, and bumping"—"than for any other activities." The Index shows that, indeed, the Dictionary contains 50 words meaning 'have sex', 49 words meaning 'drunk', and 31 words meaning 'vomit'—but there are also 45 words for 'good', for instance.

➤ For more information about the organization and use of the Index, see the About the Index (page 212) section.

Offensiveness

➤ Separate studies by several members of the slang seminar indicate that many people, both students and nonstudents, react very strongly to certain items in our Dictionary. When we began compiling the list, it contained mainly neutral or inoffensive words, but after a few weeks words were added that struck some class members as potentially offensive to other people. While we wanted our Dictionary to present an accurate picture of the full range of college concerns and vocabulary, we did not want to appear to endorse words that might be considered racist or sexist, for example, and therefore upsetting to some readers. Identifying such entries, appreciating their impact, and deciding how to mark them in the Dictionary occasioned repeated discussion in the seminar and our later editorial meetings.

➤ We decided that it is important to distinguish words that are potentially offensive only because of their subject matter (such as most words for the sex organs or for sexual intercourse, or obviously lighthearted expressions such as **do a fruit salad** 'expose one's genitals'; in general, these are not specially marked) from words that are inherently offensive to some hearers, either in any use (such as almost any expression containing **fuck**) or in a particular sense (**bitch** applied to a woman is considered offensive; as 'to complain' or as part of the expression **sit bitch** 'ride in the middle of the backseat', however, it is not). In our Dictionary we have specially marked words that are offensive in this sense with angled brackets ($< >$). Such words should generally be used with discretion in conversation with people one doesn't know well. When only certain uses of a word or expression are potentially offensive, just those definitions are marked; if every use of the word or expression should be used with caution, the entry itself is enclosed in $< >$. We have tried to be especially careful to mark words that may be offensive to members of various minority groups: interestingly, these words, and words considered sexist, seem to arouse far more emotional response among UCLA students surveyed, and the members of our class, than do the traditional four-letter words on the list. Certainly, however, other people's judgments about the potential offensiveness of many words we list might vary from ours.

➤ Our consideration of offensiveness and the way we mark it was guided by Chapman's treatment of this subject: he marks two levels of offensiveness, with the "strongest impact" rating indicating a "taboo" expression, and the "lesser impact" rating a "vulgar" one (1986: xxxiii). We experimented with marking several different levels of offensiveness, but felt that our judgments in this matter were especially arbitrary, so we have marked only one level. It is important to reiterate that our indications of offensiveness generally relate only to words and expressions, not to concepts: in some contexts, any word for, say, a private part of the body will be offensive; we have marked such a word as potentially offensive only if the use of that particular word might offend in a context where its meaning would be appropriate. There are two exceptions to this general statement, however, concepts that aroused such strong feeling among the members of our group and readers of the first version of the dictionary that they are invariably marked as offensive: these include all slang terms for homosexuality and any term referring to rape (such as **just-raped look** 'trampy, provocative style of dressing').

Slang Grammar

➤ While considering what to put in our Dictionary, we became aware of some features of what might be called "slang syntax." Since these involve grammatical constructions rather than specific words and phrases, they are not listed in our Dictionary, but several such characteristics may be mentioned briefly as part of our description of slang speech.

➤ The first of these is quite mysterious, and involves an unusual affective use of the definite article **the** that seems quite distinct from its use in standard English. Here are some examples, taken from the Dictionary:

Susan set me up with her big brother. She's the homie. [See **homie.**]
I have the mega headache. [See **mega.**]

The second sentence in the first example means something like 'She's a real homie', but does not imply that Susan is the only homie in the speaker's frame of reference. The second means about the same as 'I have a mega headache', but may be somewhat more emphatic. Thus, the use of **the** in these examples seems more emphatic than definite. **The** seems to be used the same way in such fixed expressions as **the shake** 'an undesirable person'.

➤ A second feature of slang grammar is a frequent omission of copular *be* in present-tense predicative sentences like

You crazy.

This omission of the copula almost certainly reflects the comparable omission of *be* in Black English, and illustates another influence of Black English on college slang.

➤ A final special construction involves a special use of the word **total,** whose usual college slang meaning is 'complete' or 'completely', as in

My blind date turned out to be a total barney.
I'm total hungry.

Total can also be used before a singular noun without an article, as in

Julie is total skank.

Since this sentence looks like the previous one, it initially suggested to us that the predicative word in such sentences—here, the noun **skank**—might (also?) be an adjective like *hungry*. However, **skank** cannot be used attributively (before a noun) or predicatively either alone or preceded by adverbs like *very;* since these tests fail, it is difficult to analyze *skank* as an adjective. The expression **total skank**, in contrast, seems more like *all boy* in a standard sentence like *He's all boy.*

➤ Three students surveyed aspects of the syntax of slang expressions from our Dictionary in their term papers for the slang seminar. Lori Dennis and Lauren Mendelsohn considered the grammar of adjectives, particularly whether they could occur both attributively (before a noun) and predicatively (following copular *be*), and whether they could be used in comparative *(-er)* and superlative *(-est)* form. Standard English adjectives also vary similarly along these dimensions, and these surveys validated the identification of certain words on our list as adjectives.

➤ Veli Lehman carefully studied the difference between two types of transitive verb phrases in our Dictionary, verb-preposition and verb-particle expressions. A verb-preposition expression consists of a verb followed by a preposition; the preposition and its object form a prepositional phrase. Examples from our list include **blow at** 'to yell at', **cap on** 'to insult', and **fuck with** 'to deceive'. Many such expressions occur in our Dictionary: in particular, **on** seems to be used in UCLA slang as a transitivizer: thus, for instance, **flake** is 'to cancel an appointment without notice', and **flake on** is its transitive equivalent, 'to cancel on'; **pig out** is 'to eat a lot', an intransitive verb, and **pig out on** is the transitive verb 'to eat a lot of'.

➤ Verb-particle expressions often look like verb-preposition expressions, but their syntactic characteristics are very different. In a verb-particle expression like **blow off** 'to ignore', the preposition-like word **off** (which linguists would identify as a particle) plus a following object do not form a fixed phrase. Veli's examples like *Dude, don't blow off Julie. / Dude, don't blow Julie off.* show that the object in a verb-particle expression may occur either before or after the particle. Further, pronominal objects of verb-particle expressions must occur before the particle:

Dude, don't blow her off. / *Dude, don't blow off her.

(Linguists use an asterisk before expressions that are ungrammatical or unacceptable.) These tests clearly differentiate verb-particle expressions from verb-preposition phrases, whose syntax is completely different:

I flaked on Matt. / *I flaked Matt on.
I flaked on him. / *I flaked him on.

➤ Veli found that **at, on,** and **with** were used as prepositions in expressions in our list, while **down, off, out, over,** and **up** were consistently used as particles, so the form of an expression can generally be used as a guide to usage. Finally, she discovered one expression that may be used either as a verb-preposition or a verb-particle, **dog on.** As a verb-preposition expression, **dog on** means 'to talk badly about, criticize':

We dogged on him. / *We dogged him on. 'We talked badly about him.'

As a verb-particle expression, **dog on** means 'to lead on':

She dogged him on. / *She dogged on him. 'She led him on.'

As Veli noted, the last expression is correct with a different meaning, 'She criticized him.' Standard English also has expressions that are similarly ambiguous between verb-preposition and verb-particle interpretations: thus, for example, *blow up* is a verb-preposition expression in *The wind blew up the canyon* and a verb-particle expression in *I blew up the balloon / I blew the balloon up.*

➤ The usage and meaning of college slang expressions are governed by strict principles, just as those of standard English are. The three studies reported here show that even fairly obscure facts about the grammar and lexicon of standard English have counterparts in college slang. Almost all UCLA students have a full command of standard English (which they use in writing papers and talking with older people), of course, as well as of the specialized vocabulary we have exemplified in this Dictionary. Their speech is the richer for it. We hope that this Dictionary will not only amuse them, but will help introduce other readers (in particular, their parents and professors!) to the nuances of their slang vocabulary.

Notes to the Introduction

➤ 1. Lisa Ellzey and Elaine Kealer, enthusiastic participants in the first editorial phase, were studying abroad in 1990, and did not participate in producing this revised edition of the Dictionary. All other members of the editorial group came to one or more of the 1990 meetings. Katherine Sarafian was especially helpful in encouraging and assisting the revision process.

➤ 2. Many seminar members' term papers contributed to the Dictionary in various ways. In addition to those discussed in the Slang Grammar section of this Introduction, papers by Florencia Aranovich (words for women), Deborah Creighton (words for sex), Michelle Futterman (words for drunkenness), Diana Geraci (words referring to parties), Ari Goldstein (offensive words), Sharon Kaye (offensive words), Joe Mendoza (surfing terms), Albert Nicholson (African-American slang), Kelley Poleynard (words for vomiting), and Lorna Profant (offensive words) were most influential.

➤ 3. For more on the metaphor of destruction in words for 'drunk', see Eble (1980).

➤ 4. Eble (1979) calls the process of forming "acronyms" from letters pronounced separately "initialism"; Algeo (1980) refers to such words as "alphabetisms." English spelling does not normally differentiate these from the pronounceable type of acronym, so one must know the word to guess its pronunciation. Our convention makes the pronunciation of each acronymic formation clear: thus, in our Dictionary style we would write *U.C.L.A.* (in defiance of normal University custom), since the four letters in the name of the school are pronounced separately. Interestingly, when my father attended UCLA over 50 years ago, a UCLA student was often called a *UCLAn* "yooclan" [yúklǝn], a word which can appropriately be written (in our style) without periods.

➤ One exception to the spelling rule given here is **mc**^{2} 'overly studious', which is discussed on page 7 in the Introduction. We write this word with lowercase letters and no periods because of the familiarity of the equation $e = mc^2$ (of course, a special pronunciation note appears in the text for any exceptional or doubtful cases).

The Dictionary
—

Aa

a __ and a half a real (noun) | She's a bitch and a half.

absolute real, true, total | He's an absolute babe.

ace 1. to do very well on. 2. to get rid of | I studied all week for my midterm today, and I just know I aced it. [C1 college students: 'to make a perfect or nearly perfect score'; U84]

adonis 1. extremely nice-looking, breathtaking (of a male). 2. extremely nice-looking young man | He is so adonis! | What an adonis!

ADONIS

__ -age presence or action of (verb)-ing | As we drove by a couple making out on the sidewalk, Mark pointed and said, "Ooh, neckage!" | Oh, man, there's some spillage on the foosball table. | There is some ralphage in the bathroom.

aggro hotheaded, aggressive; wild, unpredictable | He's such an aggro skater. [< aggressive. See also **go aggro**.]

AIDS for Grades AIDS and Other Sexually Transmitted Diseases (Biology 40)

airhead person who is unintelligent, gullible, naive, superficial, lacking in

AIRHEAD

< > marks words or usages that may be offensive to some or all speakers and that therefore should be used only with discretion; C = Chapman's *New Dictionary of American Slang*; U = previously collected UCLA slang. See the Introduction for more discussion. The Pronunciation Guide provides an explanation of the symbols used in phonetic transcriptions.

common sense, or *ditzy* [C3: 'stupid or silly person';
U83, 84]

➤ **airheaded** behaving like an airhead, *ditzy* [C3]

all see **be all**

all over see **be all over, freak on**

all-nighter see **pull an all-nighter**

amped high on cocaine or coffee

and a half see **a __ and a half**

animal wild, crazy person | Scott is such
an animal, never a dull moment with him!
[C5 Army & students 1940s: 'brutal or aggressive person']

appointment see **go to the doctor**

ANIMAL

arctic cold (of the weather); mean, cold (of a per-
son) | It is arctic outside. It must be less than thirty
degrees. | That was arctic of her.
➤ **Arctic!** It's cold! | Brr—arctic!

arrest to accuse (someone) of dressing unfashion-
ably, criticize (someone's) dress (usually not to his
or her face) | What an outfit! Arrest that girl! [See
also **make a fashion arrest.**]

<art fag> extremely *artsy fartsy* per-
son [C127: fag 'male homosexual']

ART FAG

artsy / artsy fartsy looking or acting
in a certain individualistic way with

many of the following characteristics: wearing black, flowing, or very tight clothing; wearing long coats, combat boots or spurs, a distinctive hairstyle, or round wire-rimmed glasses (often nonprescription); having an esoteric philosophical orientation; thinking that one has an aura [C7 1940s: 'pretentiously and self-consciously artistic']

A.S.A.F.P. as soon as possible, or sooner [< as soon as fucking possible; C7: asap]

asexual apparently uninterested in sex or dating | I was hoping that Tim would invite me to the prom, but I hadn't realized he was so asexual.

ass 1. jerk, dumb person. 2. one's self; by extension, one's responsibility or reputation | You are an ass, John. | Get your ass over here! | Your ass is on the line. [C7: 'the buttocks, posterior'. See also **badass, be on (someone's) ass, be (someone's) ass, blow smoke up (someone's) ass, haul ass, have (someone's) ass, off one's ass, tight-ass.**]

ASEXUAL

ass gasket paper protector put on a toilet seat

<**assface**> jerk, stupid person | My next door neighbor is a real assface. He knows I sleep late on Saturdays, but he still blasts his radio every morning at seven.

< > marks words or usages that may be offensive to some or all speakers and that therefore should be used only with discretion; C = Chapman's *New Dictionary of American Slang*; U = previously collected UCLA slang. See the Introduction for more discussion. The Pronunciation Guide provides an explanation of the symbols used in phonetic transcriptions.

asshole rude, obnoxious person; mean, cruel person | That cop was a major asshole —he gave me a ticket for jaywalking. [C7: 'fool, idiot']

ASSHOLE

<**asswipe**> jerk, idiot | Sometimes Mark can act like such an asswipe. I don't know why I hang out with him. [C8]

atomic atmosphere malodorous air caused by a recent fart | Mark farted and left the room, leaving in his wake an atomic atmosphere for all to enjoy.

attire see **Monday night attire**

attitude / tude bad, hostile, snobbish, or generally unpleasant attitude or behavior | She has a total attitude. [C8 black & prison: attitude 'resentful and hostile manner', C447 teenagers fr black: ATTITUDE tude 'attitude . . . usually negative'. See also **throw attitude.**]
➤ **Attitude!** (comment on someone with an attitude)

Aunt Flo one's menstrual period | I'm so mad! I wanted to go to the beach today and swim but Aunt Flo dropped in unexpectedly.

awesome outstanding | That was the most awesome concert I'd been to in a while. [C9 teenagers; U83, 84. See also **T.F.A.**]

ax see **old battle-ax**

Bb

B.A. / hang a B.A. to expose one's buttocks in a socially unacceptable context | That guy just hung a B.A. right in front of my mom! [<bare ass; U90: B.A.]
➤ **B.A.** exposed buttocks

babe 1. attractive person. 2. *dude* (term of address) | The guy who models for that store is a babe. [C11: 'a girl or woman, esp a sexually desirable one'; U84]

babe magnet person or thing (for instance, an article of clothing) that attracts members of the opposite sex. | Wow, Lorna, that skirt is a real babe magnet.

Babylon the place where sexy women *(babes)* originate or are located (pronounced [bǽbʊlan] as expected, or [bébʊlan], like "baby" plus "lawn") | Oh, wow, what a babe—she must be from Babylon.

bad good looking, *tough, hot* [C12 esp teenagers fr jazz musicians & black fr early 1950s: 'good, excellent'; U83, 84: 'good, very good'. See also **like five miles of bad road.**]

badass 1. very good, incredible, *awesome.* 2. bad, tough. 3. tough guy; cocky, troublesome person | Our new uniforms are so badass! I can't wait until

< > marks words or usages that may be offensive to some or all speakers and that therefore should be used only with discretion; C = Chapman's *New Dictionary of American Slang*; U = previously collected UCLA slang. See the Introduction for more discussion. The Pronunciation Guide provides an explanation of the symbols used in phonetic transcriptions.

our first game. | Mark thinks he is such a badass, but he's a total wimp. [C12 black: 'belligerent and worthless person' (adj)]

bag 1. to take far away, kidnap (intending to abandon as part of a fraternity prank). 2. kidnapping (as part of a fraternity prank) | Last night we bagged Mark and left him in San Diego. | The bag is on for tonight. [C13: 'get or capture'; see also **Pull a clue out of the clue bag! sleazebag**]

bag on to talk badly about, to criticize (often in a humorous style) | Sara, would you please stop bagging on me. First you criticized my hair, then my outfit, and now my taste in friends. | We guys got together last night and bagged on each other. It was fun.

bag rays / bag some rays to get a suntan, lie in the sun | We were just kicking it, bagging some rays because there weren't any waves. [C13: bag some rays 'sunbathe'; U84]

BAG RAYS

Bag that! Forget that!

bagger clumsy person, stupid person, jerk, ugly person | You bagger. I can't believe you tripped and fell in front of the whole class. [U90; See also **one bagger, two bagger.**]

bail 1. to leave. 2. to break up with, abandon | I don't feel like going to class today. Let's bail. | I bailed my girlfriend last night because she was

being totally lame. [C13 college students: 'to leave';
U83, 87]

➤ **bail on** 1. to break a date with, stand up. 2. to
gossip about, tease, criticize

bake see **fake-bake**

baked 1. high on marijuana. 2. sun-
burned or very tan | I don't understand
how he goes to class baked and still gets
good grades! | After lying in the sun for
five hours I was totally baked.

BAKED

ball 1. to have sex. 2. to have sex with | Mark balled
Kathy. Kathy balled Mark. [C14]

ball buster girl who is a tease | Carol
dresses like she wants some, but she is
such a ball buster. [C14: 'castrating female']

BALL BUSTER

balls see **blue balls, __'s balls are
hot!**

Balls out! Go! *Go for it!* | Michelle, we're late. It's a
yellow light—balls out! [C15 car-racing & motorcy-
clists: balls-out 'very great, extreme, total'. See also
go balls out, go balls out on.]

banana see **orange banana**

barf 1. to vomit. 2. vomit | Oh, sick! He just barfed
on my shoe! [C17 chiefly students]

<> marks words or usages that may be offensive to some or all speakers and that therefore
should be used only with discretion; C = Chapman's *New Dictionary of American Slang*; U =
previously collected UCLA slang. See the Introduction for more discussion. The Pronunciation
Guide provides an explanation of the symbols used in phonetic transcriptions.

➤ **barfola** see **-ola**

barking spiders audible fart (usually used as an exclamation) | What was that? Barking spiders!

barney person who's not with it, *nerd* (especially, white nerd); ugly guy | My blind date turned out to be a total barney. [<Barney, a character in "The Flintstones"]

base on to criticize

bathtub scum see **shower scum**

BARNEY

battle-ax see **old battle-ax**

B.A.V. person who has not had sex in an unusually long period of time [<born again virgin]

be after some see **want some**

be all 1. to say. 2. to go like (with a gesture) | He was all, "That guy's a fag." So I told him to fuck off. | Then she was all (gesture made by flipping hair). Sometimes that girl makes me ill. [U87: 'be always saying']

be all over to do; to get absorbed in | After the boss demanded the report by noon, the employee was all over it.

be beat with an ugly stick / be slapped with an ugly stick / be whipped with an ugly stick to be ugly, become ugly (often used as a reason for why someone should be ugly) | So how did the Mike

Tyson lookalike get to be so ugly? She was beat with an ugly stick. [See also **beat (someone) with an ugly stick.**]

be dragging to feel ill or lethargic | I drank so much last night that I'm dragging big time. [C8: one's ass is dragging 'one is exhausted and hence sluggish']

be dust to be ruined, fatigued, finished | If you don't show up, you're dust! [U84; See also **dust.**]

be golden be perfect; be doing well, be in perfect shape | As soon as I get caught up on my homework, I'll be golden.

be hanging big bootie out to be in the way: especially, to park one's car in such a way that a significant portion of it is blocking a driveway | After driving around for 20 minutes looking for a parking space, Jennifer finally just parked in front of our apartment, but she was hanging big bootie out. [C40 esp black: booty 'the sex act; sex; ass'. See also **Hang a bootie!**]

BE GOLDEN

be hating life / be hating it / be hating to be despondent; to be in an unfortunate situation or condition | Oh, wow, he's hating—he's got three papers due tomorrow. | That carpet's hating it. [See also **be loving life.**]

be having a drought see **be in a drought**

< > marks words or usages that may be offensive to some or all speakers and that therefore should be used only with discretion; C = Chapman's *New Dictionary of American Slang*; U = previously collected UCLA slang. See the Introduction for more discussion. The Pronunciation Guide provides an explanation of the symbols used in phonetic transcriptions.

be history to be finished, in trouble; to have had someone break up with one | My boyfriend broke up with me and now I'm history. [See also **hist, histed.**]

be illin to be in a bad or unfortunate situation; to react inappropriately; to act stupid | He was illin when he found out he didn't pass his philosophy class. [U87: illin' 'stupid']

be in a drought / be having a drought to have a long period with no dates or sexual contact | Steve hasn't had a date in months—he's in a serious drought. [See also **bootie drought.**]

<be in (someone's) crack> to be nosy about (someone), be too involved in (someone's) business [C85: crack 'the deep crease between the buttocks']

be in (someone's) face to bother (someone, especially someone very nearby), to fight with (someone) | He was totally in her face. [C162: get out of someone's face 'leave alone, stop annoying'. See also **Get out of my face!**]

BE IN
(SOMEONE'S)
FACE

be in the ditch to be really drunk

be in there / be right in there to be pleased and excited, to be *stoked* | You passed your driver's test? You're in there! [C228: in there 'making a great effort, coping energetically and successfully'; U84]

be into to enjoy, be involved in, be interested in | I used to be into writing music but now I don't have the time. | I'm really into him.

be laying pipe to have sex | Where was Bob last night during the party? Oh, he was laying pipe in his bedroom. [C255 black: lay pipe 'to do the sex act']

be like to say | He asked me to go dancing, and I'm like, "I have a boyfriend, you know."

be loving life / be loving it to be in a good or fortunate situation or condition [See also **be hating life.**]

be married to have a serious relationship, be seriously dating

be on a mission to be looking for | We're on a mission for a cool bar and some fine dudes!

BE MARRIED

<be on my jock> to be persistently pursuing me (especially sexually; used by a male speaker) | That chick calls me every night. She's always on my jock. [C237 late 1700s British: jock 'penis'; C304: on someone's back 'persistently pursuing or harassing'. See also **be on my tit.**]

<be on my tit> to be persistently pursuing me (especially sexually; used by a female speaker)

< > **marks words or usages that may be offensive to some or all speakers and that therefore should be used only with discretion; C = Chapman's** *New Dictionary of American Slang;* **U = previously collected UCLA slang. See the Introduction for more discussion. The Pronunciation Guide provides an explanation of the symbols used in phonetic transcriptions.**

[C304: on someone's back 'persistently pursuing or harassing'. See also **be on my jock.**]

be on (someone's) ass to bother (someone), to tailgate (someone) in a car [? C304: on one's ass 'in a sad or helpless condition']

be out of here to be on the point of leaving (so quickly that one has virtually already left—usually used in the present tense) | I've got a class in

BE OUT OF HERE

ten minutes, you guys—I'm out of here. [See also **be out of there.**]

be out of there to have left (usually used in past tense) [See also **be out of here.**]

be over to be sick and tired of | I was over that class when the professor didn't show up repeatedly.

be raked / get raked to do badly, be humiliated, be emotionally or intellectually strained or exhausted (especially by something external), to have undergone a grueling experience; to lose (in a game) | That test was horrible! I got raked! [C196: rake someone over the coals 'put someone through an ordeal'. See also **rake on.**]

Be real! / Get real! Be sensible! Come back to reality! | —John, are you going fishing this weekend? —Be real, Smitty, I have to study for a test.

be single to not be involved in a relationship | He's been single a long time.

be (someone's) ass to be (someone's) downfall, to be the end of (someone) | This paper will be my ass if I don't turn it in. [C229: it will be someone's ass 'that will be the end or ruination of someone']

be sprung on to have a crush on | Lisa is so sprung on Mark—I think she's planning her winter schedule so that she has two classes with him.

be talking with to be going with, to be dating steadily | Are you talking with him?

BE SPRUNG ON

be there to plan to be in a certain place, to really want to go to a certain event (normally follows a mention of the place or event) | Michael Jackson is giving a concert at the Forum. I'm there!

be ticking to talk in class without being prepared, to *B.S.* in class

be to the curb to vomit | —What's Mark doing? — Oh, he's to the curb. He drank too much.

be up to no good to engage in sexual activity

beastmaster guy who consistently dates ugly girls [C19: beast 'especially unattractive woman']

beat 1. very ugly. 2. stupid, *lame* | That chick is so beat that she's been mistaken for Mike Tyson. [C19: 'looking as if battered', 'inferior']

< > marks words or usages that may be offensive to some or all speakers and that therefore should be used only with discretion; C = Chapman's *New Dictionary of American Slang;* U = previously collected UCLA slang. See the Introduction for more discussion. The Pronunciation Guide provides an explanation of the symbols used in phonetic transcriptions.

beat (someone) with an ugly stick to have sex with (someone) [See also **be beat with an ugly stick.**]

beau 1. stupid person, clumsy person, *geek*. 2. boyfriend [See also **beauhunk.**]

beauhunk 1. boyfriend. 2. *studly* looking guy, especially one with a seventies appearance | I'm going to the beach with my beauhunk. [<beau + hunk. See also **beau.**]

beddy promiscuous girl [see also **betty**]

beef see **slip (someone) the hot beef injection**

beemer B.M.W. car | I have always wanted a red beemer. I think they are the classiest cars.

beer bong device consisting of a funnel attached to a tube for drinking beer quickly [See also **do a beer bong.**]

beer goggles blurry vision resulting from too many drinks, which makes everyone of the opposite sex look very appealing | After a few drinks Arnold had beer goggles and suddenly every girl at the bar was looking good. [See also **coke bottle eyes.**]

BEER GOGGLES

beige boring | My date talked about his stamp collection the whole night. What a beige personality! [C21 high school students]

believer gullible person

bells see **Hell's bells!**

bend over to get messed up, *screwed* | He might as well ask me to bend over.

➤ **Bend over! / B.O.!** You're bothering me! You *suck! Get a life!*

bent demented, acting strange or weird | You are so bent. I can't believe that you partied all night, even though you have a midterm today. [?C23 Air Force Academy: 'upset'; 'intoxicated'; 'sexually aberrant'; 'dishonest']

bertha overweight girl [C24: Big Bertha 'large or fat woman']

betty pretty girl (used by males) | The girl in Abnormal Psychology is a definite betty. [<Betty, a character in "The Flint-stones." See also **beddy**.]

Betty rub! You're gonna get lucky! (in a sexual sense—used between males)

BETTY

B.F.D. Big deal! So what! | I got another C on my math test—B.F.D.! [<big fucking deal; C23: 'something or someone of importance']

B.F.E. / B.F.A. the boondocks, a very far away place | No one wants to take Troy home because he lives out in B.F.E. [<Butt Fucking Egypt, Butt Fucking Africa; C51 Army: Bumfuck, Egypt 'a very distant and remote place'. See also **Bumblefuck**.]

biddy bothersome old woman [C24]

< > marks words or usages that may be offensive to some or all speakers and that therefore should be used only with discretion; C = Chapman's *New Dictionary of American Slang;* U = previously collected UCLA slang. See the Introduction for more discussion. The Pronunciation Guide provides an explanation of the symbols used in phonetic transcriptions.

biff 1. dumb, dunce-like girl. 2. to fail. 3. to go to the bathroom | That girl is such a biff, and she isn't even in a sorority. | My chemistry midterm was impossible. I totally biffed it. [?C24 musicians: 'missed high note on a brass instrument']

➤ **biffy** portable toilet [C24 chiefly Canadian: 'toilet']

big bootie out see **be hanging big bootie out**

big hair / big Texas hair teased hair

Big shit! big deal; so what? | After Julie told Tara her great news, Tara replied, "Big shit!"

big time totally and completely | He's head over heels for that girl. Big time. | I was big time in love with her. [C26]

big white phone see **talk to Ralph on the big white phone**

big X see **the big X**

biggie see **No biggie!**

bill see **monthly bill**

bip to hit

bird see **give (someone) the bird**

biscuit gullible person

bison to vomit [See also **water buffalo, yak.**]

BIP

bitch <1. cruel, evil, or rude person (normally used about women, but may also be used about men).> 2. unfortunate situation, very difficult or tedious thing. 3. to complain, gripe. <4. girl a guy dates (often used in the plural).> 5. middle seat in the back of a car | My English teacher is such a bitch! She gave me a C− on my paper! | Waiting in line for concert tickets was a total bitch; it took three hours. | I bitched about having to get up early on a Saturday morning. | She's one of my bitches. [(1, 2, 3) C28. See also **bushbitch, flip a bitch, No bitch! ride bitch.**]

BITCH

bitchin good, excellent, *rad* | That is a bitchin surfboard. It is so nice it must have cost a fortune. [C28]

bite 1. to copy without permission, to steal an idea. 2. to be very bad, to *suck* | Why did you bite my outfit? Now we look like twins! | Don't bite. This is my idea and I want credit for it. | It bites that I have two finals in a row tomorrow. [C28: 'to borrow money from'. See also **monkey bite.**]

BITE

<**Bite me!**> Shut up! You make me sick! Get out of here! Kiss my ass! *Fuck you!* | After Joe told Michele that he wanted to see other girls, all she said was, "Bite me!" [C29: bite my ass]

bites see **mosquito bites**

< > marks words or usages that may be offensive to some or all speakers and that therefore should be used only with discretion; C = Chapman's *New Dictionary of American Slang;* U = previously collected UCLA slang. See the Introduction for more discussion. The Pronunciation Guide provides an explanation of the symbols used in phonetic transcriptions.

biting very cold (of the weather) | Joe, you'd better bring your jacket to the game tonight. It's biting outside. [See also **nibbling.**]

bitter annoyed, frustrated, *pissed* | I am so bitter—someone called me this morning at six and it was a wrong number.

bizarre weird

blade to get rid of, *eighty-six*

blasted drunk, intoxicated | At the party Saturday we were all blasted because the punch was spiked. [C30]

BIZARRE

blitzed drunk, intoxicated | I had two of those hurricane punches last night at A.T.O. I was so blitzed that I had forgotten my address and phone number by the end of the night. [C31]

blotch to stain one's underpants with a liquid-emitting fart | James was really embarrassed when he blotched in front of his grandparents.

BLOTCH

➤ **blotcher** liquid-emitting fart that stains one's underpants | "That blotcher was so gross!" Sue said to Frank—but little did she know that he had diarrhea and couldn't help it.

blotto drunk, intoxicated | I don't want to play Quarters any more. I'm already way blotto. [C32 early 1900s]

blow 1. to vomit. 2. to sing well. <3. to give a blow job to.> 4. to have sex with. 5. cocaine. (The past of the first three verbs is "blew"; "blowed" may be used as the past in meaning 4.) | He blowed her. | The M.F. proba-

BLOW

bly stole my radio to score some blow. [(3) C32; (2) C32 esp 1950s beat & cool talk: 'do or perform something . . . well'. See also **blow chunks.**]

blow at to yell at, especially to yell orders at constantly | The camp counselors had had enough— they had listened to the camp staff blow at them all week long.

blow away to amaze, shock | The test was so hard it totally blew me away. [C33; U83]

blow chunks / blow chow / blow cookies to vomit | If I don't get some air, I'm gonna blow chow. | If you're going to blow cookies, get out of the car! [U83, 84, 87: blow chunks. See also **toss one's cookies.**]

BLOW CHUNKS

blow jaw to smoke marijuana [C32: blow 'smoke marijuana']

blow off to ignore, skip | Because it looked like it would be a perfect day at the beach, Mark decided to blow off class. | Dude, don't blow Julie off! [C33: 'to avoid or shirk'; U83, 84, 87]

< > marks words or usages that may be offensive to some or all speakers and that therefore should be used only with discretion; C = Chapman's *New Dictionary of American Slang*; U = previously collected UCLA slang. See the Introduction for more discussion. The Pronunciation Guide provides an explanation of the symbols used in phonetic transcriptions.

blow smoke up (someone's) ass to try to deceive or impress (someone) | I was late because I had a flat tire, but my dad thought I was just blowing smoke up his ass.

blown drunk, intoxicated; high or *wired* on drugs

BLOWN

blue balls painful condition of the testicles due to unfulfilled sexual excitement | Harold said he has blue balls; he was with Priscilla last night. [C34]

bluehaired <elderly person (usually female)> | Do you see the wide right turn that bluehaired just made? [See also **grayhaired.**]

B.O.! see **Bend over!**

boag to vomit (pronounced [bóg]— rhymes with "vogue") | After running the race on a full stomach, he boaged. [?C36 high school students: bogue 'disgusting, unattractive']

BOAG

Bob see **Hi, Bob!**

bobo drunk, intoxicated

bodacious very *cool,* appealing [<*Bill and Ted's Excellent Adventure;* C36 chiefly southern fr middle 1800s: bodacious 'extreme']

➤ **bodacious tatas** big or appealing breasts [<*An Officer and a Gentleman*]

BODACIOUS
TATAS

boff 1. to have sex. 2. to have sex with | It was only our first date but I boffed her anyway. [C36; U84]

bogus ridiculous, unfair, unbelievable | That was so bogus when the cop pulled Mark over for turning on a yellow. [C36 teenagers: 'ignorant, not up-to-date, unattractive'; U83: 'excellent, good, great'; 84: 'no good, bad repulsive'; 87: 'false']

boink 1. to have sex. 2. to have sex with | Tom boinked his girlfriend.

bolt to leave quickly | I am really late for class. I have to bolt.

BOLT

bomb to fail, do poorly on | My chemistry final was so hard that I totally bombed it. [C37; U84]

bombed drunk, intoxicated | I was so bombed at last night's party that I needed two people to get me home. [C37]

BOMBED

bone <1. to have sex.> <2. to have sex with> [C37: 'the erect penis'. See also **boner, do the bone dance, give (someone) the bird.**]

bonehead 1. dope, moron. 2. stupid, slow-paced | I can't believe you sat through half of a physics class thinking it was calculus. You're such a bonehead! [C37]

BONEHEAD

> marks words or usages that may be offensive to some or all speakers and that therefore should be used only with discretion; C = Chapman's *New Dictionary of American Slang;* U = previously collected UCLA slang. See the Introduction for more discussion. The Pronunciation Guide provides an explanation of the symbols used in phonetic transcriptions.

boner erection [<bone + er; C37. See also **have a C.B.**]

bones dollars | —How much was your watch? —Thirty-five bones. [C37. See also **jump on (someone's) bones.**]

bong see **beer bong, do a beer bong**

Bonnie Brillo someone very clean and neat | There is not a speck of dust in the living room. Bonnie Brillo must've cleaned today. [See also **Brillohead.**]

BONNIE BRILLO

Bonus! Great! | Bonus, dude! [U90]

boofa stupid person, *loser, dork* (pronounced [búfə], like "boo" plus "fa" as in "sofa") | Jimmy's such a boofa! All he does is waste time playing with his Rubik's cube; he doesn't even speak!

BONUS!

boofed puffed out, bouffant (usually, of a hairdo; pronounced [búft]—rhymes with "poofed") | After she got a perm, Jan's hair was totally boofed. [<bouffant, perhaps influenced by poofed]

boogers see **eye boogers**

boogie 1. to go. 2. to do quickly (pronounced [bʊ́gi], with "boo-" as in "book") | Let's boogie. This party is really dead. | I need to boogie on this paper —it's due tomorrow. [U83: 'go somewhere']

book to leave or go quickly | I'm already fifteen minutes late for class. I'd better book! [C39 students; U83, 84, 87]

book smart academically intelligent but lacking common sense, common knowledge, or social skills; absentminded | That girl is really book smart—she gets straight As, but she forgot she had to enroll for next quarter's classes this week.

BOOK SMART

books see **crack the books**

boost to have sex with | He boosted her. | She boosted him.

boot to vomit | Dude, I can't even hang. I only drank three beers before I booted. [?C40: 'to lose or waste by incompetence . . .']

bootie see **be hanging big bootie out, Hang a bootie!**

bootie drought lack of sex | Why are you acting so strange, Sheila? Do you have bootie drought? [C40 esp black: booty 'the sex act, sex'. See also **be in a drought.**]

boots see **fuck-me boots, knock boots with**

booyah wham, bang, crack (pronounced [búya], "boo" plus "yah") | The car hit us and booyah, my head flew into the windshield. | After that booyah, Mike's head was spinning.

boss great, *awesome* | That concert last night was boss! [C41 teenagers, fr black & jazz musicians; U83 ("old"), 84]

bottle see **coke bottle eyes**

bottom to drink down, finish drinking | Bottom it and we'll go.

BOSS

bow to the porcelain god / bow to the porcelain goddess to vomit into the toilet

bowhead girl who always wears bows in her hair; girl who plays close attention to the way she looks | The bowhead was miffed when she lost her mascara.

BOWHEAD

bowl see **smoke a bowl**

box portable stereo | Dude! Turn down your box! [See also **skanky box.**]

boy see **buttboy, frat rat, homeboy**

brain-dead stupid, unable to think

BRAIN-DEAD

Brainfart! (exclamation used about a sudden loss of memory or train of thought, or a sudden inability to think logically) | In the middle of his sentence he blanked out— "... which leads directly to my ... uh ... brainfart!" [<brain + fart]

brat see **frat brat**

break out with / bust out with to do, wear, or say (something unexpected and bold, or very good looking); to surprisingly or suddenly produce (something new and unexpected) | Look at Shelly, she's trying to break out with her new outfit. | Everyone at the party was bummed because there was no more beer. Then Lauren broke out with a six-pack.

breeder adult heterosexual (mainly used by homosexuals) | She has pretty good taste for a breeder. [C45; U83]

BREEDER

brew see **shock a brew**

brewhaha / brewha / haha / ha can of beer, drink of beer [<brew + haha/brouhaha; C45: brew]

brewhound person who loves to get drunk (not necessarily an alcoholic) | Many frat guys are brewhounds.

brewsky can of beer, drink of beer [C45: brewskie]

BREWHOUND

brick 1. mess, failure. 2. to fail, receive a failing grade. 3. to fail on, receive a failing grade on | I really bricked that paper. | That shot didn't even hit the rim—it was a real brick! [C116: drop a brick 'to blunder'; U84: 'failure']

< > marks words or usages that may be offensive to some or all speakers and that therefore should be used only with discretion; C = Chapman's *New Dictionary of American Slang;* U = previously collected UCLA slang. See the Introduction for more discussion. The Pronunciation Guide provides an explanation of the symbols used in phonetic transcriptions.

brickhouse big-chested woman | Dolly Parton is a brickhouse. [C50: built like a brick shithouse]

Brillohead person with very coarse hair | Our apartment manager was a Brillohead. [See also **Bonnie Brillo.**]

bring down to depress, to upset, to constantly ruin (someone's) good mood | My roommate always brings me down with her loud obnoxious attitude. | I think I bring her down when I talk about my problems so much. [C45]

broomhilda short, ugly girl [<the comic strip character]

brownnose 1. to be extra nice to, to *kiss up to* 2. person who brownnoses, curries favor, or flatters in order to gain approval | Rich brownnosed the teacher. When grades come out, he will undoubtedly get an A. [C46; U83]

BROWNNOSE

➤ **brownnoser** *brownnose,* person who *brownnoses*

B.S. 1. to say or write something one doesn't know much about, to fake a response. 2. stupid nonsense | I didn't know the answer, so I had to B.S. [<bull shit; C47. See also **bullshit.**]

bub person with no redeeming qualities, *zero* | That guy has no friends because he is such a bub. [C47: 'man, fellow (used in direct address, with a slightly insulting intent)']

bubblebutt 1. large rear end with rounded buttocks. 2. person with a bubblebutt | That girl has a bubblebutt. It looks like she has a pillow in her pants.

bud marijuana | Let's smoke some bud before we go out tonight with those chicks. Otherwise I won't be able to deal with them. [C48 teenagers]
➤ **buds / budlies / budulars** marijuana (grammatically plural) | These buds are great.
➤ **budman** person who sells or has marijuana | I am going to buy some bud from the budman.

buff / buffed strong, muscular | Steve has been pumping weight all year, and now he's buff. | Joe's the buffedest guy I know. [C48: buff 'naked'; U83, 84, 87]

buffoonery ridiculous or foolish action | He got drunk and started to take his clothes off. Some buffoonery! [See also **mockery**.]

BUFF

<bufu> 1. to have anal sex with. 2. homosexual male (pronounced [búfu], like "boo" plus "foo") [<butt fuck; U84: '(heterosexual) sex, to have (heterosexual) sex with']

bug to be unhappy, irritated, impatient, and to therefore treat others poorly; to be annoying, to *suck* | Louise just came in

BUG

< > marks words or usages that may be offensive to some or all speakers and that therefore should be used only with discretion; C = Chapman's *New Dictionary of American Slang;* U = previously collected UCLA slang. See the Introduction for more discussion. The Pronunciation Guide provides an explanation of the symbols used in phonetic transcriptions.

here and yelled at everyone for no reason. Why in the world is she bugging? | Our final is on Friday—that bugs. [C49 1960s counterculture, fr black: 'to irritate or anger'; U84 'annoy']

Buick see **ride the Buick**

bullshit 1. angry, mad, *pissed off.* 2. drunk, intoxicated. 3. to say or write something one doesn't know much about, to fake a response. 4. stupid nonsense | Dude, my roommate drank all my beers! I'm so bullshit! [See also **B.S.**]

bum 1. person who ordinarily looks nice but has decided not to bother with his or her appearance. 2. to take, to borrow (something to which one's not entitled). 3. to be disappointed, depressed | This is my first day off in weeks; I'm going to be a bum and not even shave. | Can I bum a cigarette? [C51: 'drifter, vagrant, hobo'; 'to beg or borrow']

BUM

➤ **bum around** to relax, to do nothing, to hang out | After a long day on campus, I'm just going to bum around until dinnertime.

➤ **bum out** to disappoint [C51]

Bumblefuck any faraway little town [C51 Army: Bumfuck, Egypt 'a very distant and remote place'. See also **B.F.E.**]

bummed disappointed, depressed | Christie was bummed when Doug didn't show up. [C51; U83]

➤ **bummer** something disappointing or unfortunate [C51 teenagers, fr sixties counterculture: 'any bad experience or occasion; bad situation or place'; U83]

bump 1. to have sex. 2. to have sex with | He bumped her. | They bumped. [C51: 'to make pregnant']

➤ **bump fuzz** to have sex | Did you bump fuzz with Julie last night? [See also **fuzz bumper.**]

Bump that! Forget that!

bumper see **fuzz bumper**

bunged up scrunched up in an uncomfortable or abnormal way (first word pronounced [bʌ́nǰd]—rhymes with "lunged") | Jane's slip was all bunged up under her dress so she went into the bathroom to fix it.

BUNGED UP

bunk bad, no good; false, phony; boring, *lame* | That comedian thought he was funny, but he was pretty bunk. | I can't believe he stood me up—that's so bunk. [C52: 'nonsense']

burn 1. to insult, point out (someone's) shortcoming or past error or embarrassment. 2. insult

➤ **Burn!** Gotcha! Busted! (exclamation used after a burn)

➤ **burn on (someone)** insult to (someone) | That was a total burn on you.

< > marks words or usages that may be offensive to some or all speakers and that therefore should be used only with discretion; C = Chapman's *New Dictionary of American Slang;* U = previously collected UCLA slang. See the Introduction for more discussion. The Pronunciation Guide provides an explanation of the symbols used in phonetic transcriptions.

burned out exhausted, tired | Jennifer is real burned out from studying all night. [C53]
- ➤ **burned out on** sick of | I'm burned out on studying every night. [C53: burned out 'bored']
- ➤ **burn-out** dropout; *loser; stoner* [C54 teenagers: 'user or abuser of drugs, liquor, etc.']
- ➤ **burnt** tired or emotionally drained | I've done so much shit for my fraternity. I am so burnt.

burrito penis

bus see **drive the bus**

<**bushbitch**> ugly girl [<Eddie Murphy's *Raw*]

bush-league stupid, unfair, *lame* | —I didn't get housing. —That's bush-league. [C54: 'mediocre, second- or third-rate'. See also **major-league.**]

<**bushpig**> ugly girl | A girl would have to be really ugly to be called a bushpig.

BUSHPIG

bust 1. to earn, receive (a good grade). 2. to make (a difficult shot in basketball) | He busted an A on the test.
- ➤ **Bust!** (exclamation used about a difficult shot in basketball)

bust a move 1. to make a move, *go for it.* 2. to leave (*busted a move) | From the way he was eyeing that girl it was obvious that he was going to bust a move. | Oh, I'm running late—I've got to bust a move. [<"Bust a Move" by Young M.C.; (1) U90]
- ➤ **Bust a move!** Goodbye!

bust fresh to look very good on a particular occasion (perhaps unexpectedly) | On New Year's I'm going to bust fresh with the raddest dress.

bust out with see **break out with**

BUST FRESH

bust up 1. to laugh. 2. to make (someone) laugh | I started busting up after I read the first sentence of his letter. | He told a joke and totally busted us up.

buster see **ball buster**

BUST UP

busy see **get busy**

butt very, truly, extremely, very much so, incredibly | I had to get up butt early this morning for my eight o'clock class! [See also **bubblebutt, butt-ass, kick ass, kiss ass, up the butt.**]

<**butt pirate**> homosexual male | West Hollywood is full of butt pirates.

butt-ass very | It's butt-ass cold. [<butt + ass. See also **butt.**]

<**buttboy**> 1. homosexual male. 2. male jerk

butter not cool, *nerdy* | Her sandals were totally butter; they looked like they were made in 1960! [See also **cheese.**]

BUTTBOY

< > marks words or usages that may be offensive to some or all speakers and that therefore should be used only with discretion; C = Chapman's *New Dictionary of American Slang;* U = previously collected UCLA slang. See the Introduction for more discussion. The Pronunciation Guide provides an explanation of the symbols used in phonetic transcriptions.

butthead stupid person, idiot | You are such a butthead! You should have turned in your term paper on time!

butt-kicker really good person or thing | He's a real butt-kicker in soccer. [See also **kick ass.**]

➤ **butt-kicking** 1. strong and immense, powerful, huge. 2. outstanding | That bar has a **BUTT-KICKER** butt-kicking security guard who stands in the doorway every night and checks I.D.s—we'll never get in with our fake driver's licenses.

buttlick 1. idiot, jerk. 2. person who curries favor or flatters in order to gain approval; *brownnose* | That police officer is such a buttlick. He gave me a ticket for doing thirty-nine miles an hour in a thirty-five zone.

buttly extremely ugly (usually, of a person) | That guy dancing with Julie is buttly. [<u>butt</u> ug<u>ly</u>]

BUTTLY

buzz to leave in a hurry, to move quickly | I don't want that guy over there to see me, so let's buzz as soon as class is over. [?C57: buzz off 'to depart'; U83: buzz off 'get lost!' See also **buzzkill, catch a buzz, have a buzz, kill (someone's) buzz.**]

➤ **buzzed** not yet drunk, but feeling pretty good; really drunk | I was buzzed after my first three beers, and everything that happened made me want to laugh. [C57: 'intoxicated, especially mildly so']

buzzkill / buzzstomp 1. bad experience or event, downer, *bummer*. 2. bothersome person, person who ruins a good time [C57: buzz 'feeling a surge of pleasure, . . . high'. See also **kill (someone's) buzz.**]

Buzzkill! / Buzzstomp! That's too bad! What a *drag*!

Cc

C ya! see **See ya!**

cadet unappealing person, misfit, *nerd, geek* | Ignore him, he's such a cadet. [See also **space cadet.**]

cake easy | You should take that class —it's cake. [C59 college students; U90]

➤ **cake / cakewalk** easy task | This Biology 5 class is a cakewalk compared to Chemistry 11A. [C59: cakewalk; 322: piece of cake]

CAKE

call see **last call look**

camper see **happy camper**

< > marks words or usages that may be offensive to some or all speakers and that therefore should be used only with discretion; C = Chapman's *New Dictionary of American Slang;* U = previously collected UCLA slang. See the Introduction for more discussion. The Pronunciation Guide provides an explanation of the symbols used in phonetic transcriptions.

Can you say "__"? That's really (adjective)! What a (noun)! I'm really (adjective)! | I didn't get any sleep—can you say "tired"?

can't hang see **hang**

cap to say something mean or insulting | I could cap! [?C61: 'to best or outdo']
➤ **cap on** to insult, degrade, put down | Joe's friends are going to totally cap on him when they find out he is going out with a thirteen-year-old girl. [U83]

Cap'n Toke person who smokes marijuana a lot [C441: toke 'puff or drag at . . . a marijuana cigarette']

Caps drinking game in which players throw beer bottle caps into each other's glasses

Carpe diem! Follow your dream! *Go for it!* [<Latin 'seize the day', popularized in *Dead Poets Society*]

CARPE DIEM!

<carpet muncher> / <rug muncher> female homosexual [C365: rug 'toupee']

cas all right, fine, well enough; mellow (pronounced [kǽž], like the "cas" of "casual") | —Do you want to go to the movies tonight? —Okay, that's cas. [<casual; C62 teenagers: cas 'casual, informal']

case see **space cadet**

cashed physically, mentally, or financially drained | After studying for my midterm all night, I'm cashed. | —Lori, can I borrow twenty dollars? —Sorry, I just bought a new Cabriolet—I'm cashed.

CASHED

cast of characters people who are associated in some way (for instance, with a place or activity) | Did you see the cast of characters down at dinner?

catch a buzz to start feeling the effects of alcohol or another drug [C57: buzz 'a feeling or surge of pleasure, especially a pleasant sense of intoxication']

catch flack / get flack to receive negative verbal feedback [C137: flak, flack 'severe criticism'. See also **catch shit.**]

catch shit to be verbally harassed, scolded | You're going to catch shit if you miss practice. [C63: catch hell 'to be severely rebuked or punished'. See also **catch flack.**]

catch some Zs / cop some Zs to sleep | I studied for six hours so now I have to catch some Zs. [C83 black]

CATCH SOME ZS

Categories drinking game in which each player must name a new item in a specified category

< > marks words or usages that may be offensive to some or all speakers and that therefore should be used only with discretion; C = Chapman's *New Dictionary of American Slang*; U = previously collected UCLA slang. See the Introduction for more discussion. The Pronunciation Guide provides an explanation of the symbols used in phonetic transcriptions.

cavities see **give (someone) cavities, have cavities**

C.B. see **have a C.B.**

C.F.M. sexually suggestive | Her outfit was so weird. All of her other clothes were preppy, but she had a C.F.M. skirt on. [<come fuck me. See also **fuck-me boots.**]

champ see **Easy!**

champion see **"Jeopardy" champion**

characters see **cast of characters**

Check it out! / Check this out! Look at this, listen to this! Wow! *Awesome!* | Check it out! That wave is huge! | Check this out, Joe, she said she thought I was a snob. | [C66: check out 'to look closely at']

cheese something out of date or *cheesy* | That dress you're wearing is total cheese. [See also **butter, cheesy, cheez whiz, chew the cheese, fumunda cheese.**]

cheese dong stupid person | If that cheese dong makes another stupid comment I will hit him.

cheese off to *mooch* from | He's always cheesing off me.
➤ **cheeser** moocher

cheesy outdated or unfashionable enough to be brought back or imitated; trampy-looking; old-fashioned, dull (of a person); fat | After looking through her mother's old clothes, Sally decided the purple and orange polka-dot dress was so cheesy that it would be fun to wear to school. [C67: 'lacking in taste, vulgarly unesthetic; shoddy; shabby, ugly']

cheez whiz 1. out-of-date, *cheesy.* 2. something that's out-of-date or *cheesy* | Her shoes were total cheez whiz.
➤ **Cheez whiz!** Gee whiz!

chemisery chemistry [<u>chemi</u>stry + <u>misery</u>]

cherry 1. virgin. 2. in perfect condition, *sweet, awesome* | That used moped you bought is so cherry. [C66: 'virgin, of either sex'; 'in an unproved or maiden state'; U83: 'car in perfect condition'. See also **have one's cherry.**]

CHERRY

Chester Molester lecherous man

chew on to pester, nag | My boyfriend always chews on me when I go out without him: "Where are you going? Who's going with you? Are there any guys going? . . ." [? C67: chew out 'reprimand severely']

CHEW ON

chew the cheese to vomit | You're looking pretty green there. Are you sure you're not going to chew the cheese? [C66: cheese 'to vomit' (n)]

< > marks words or usages that may be offensive to some or all speakers and that therefore should be used only with discretion; C = Chapman's *New Dictionary of American Slang;* U = previously collected UCLA slang. See the Introduction for more discussion. The Pronunciation Guide provides an explanation of the symbols used in phonetic transcriptions.

chichi elegant, classy, posh (pronounced [šíši], like "she-she") | The Bistro is a very chichi restaurant. [C67: chichi 'something frilly, fancy, precious, and overdecorated' (adj)]

CHICHI

chick girl | Dude, that chick is so hot. [C68 esp beat, cool, & 1960s counterculture]

chickenshit 1. coward, *wimp*. 2. insufficient, of poor quality, *lame* | Rob, this finance report is chickenshit. [C68 WWII armed forces: chicken shit 'the rules, restrictions, rigors, and meanness of a minor and pretentious tyrant' (adj). See also **piece of chickenshit.**]

chill 1. to relax, not get upset, calm down. 2. to relax, take it easy [C68. See also **cold chill, take a chill pill.**]
- ➤ **chill out** to calm down, relax | Chill out, Andy, you'll pass the test. [C68 teenagers, fr black; U84, 87]

choice very good, excellent, very nice, great | The beach was so choice last week! | The view from Mark's tenth-floor apartment is choice.

choke to do poorly at something one should have done well at | I can't believe it —I studied all night for my test and I totally choked. I mean, the best grade I could have gotten was a C. [C70 esp sports: choke

CHOKE

up 'to become tense and ineffective under pressure']

chow! goodbye | I'll talk to you tomorrow, chow! [<Italian *ciao*]

chow / chow down to eat, have some food [C71: chow; fr Navy: chow down. See also **blow chunks.**]
➤ **chow on / chow down on** to eat (something)

CHOW

Christmas see **What is this, Christmas?**

chud disgusting, gross [<the movie *CHUD (cannibalistic humanoid underground dwellers)*]

chug to drink quickly | Let's have a chugging contest. Ready, go! [C71: 'to drink the whole of what is in a glass or bottle without pausing']

CHUD

chum the fish to vomit | David fully chummed the fish after the frat party. [C71: chum 'to throw ground-up bait into the water to attract fish'. See also **chummy.**]

CHUM THE FISH

chummy to vomit | Derek chummied all over the carpet. [See also **chum the fish.**]

< > marks words or usages that may be offensive to some or all speakers and that therefore should be used only with discretion; C = Chapman's *New Dictionary of American Slang*; U = previously collected UCLA slang. See the Introduction for more discussion. The Pronunciation Guide provides an explanation of the symbols used in phonetic transcriptions.

chunk to do badly; to vomit | I chunked on my math midterm. [See also **blow chunks.**]

circle see **square (someone's) circle**

class see **weeder**

classic worth remembering, out-standing, appropriate, funny | Today in class my professor fell off the stage —it was classic.

CLASSIC

clue see **get a clue, have a clue, Pull a clue out of the clue bag! have negative clues**
➤ **Clue in!** Pay attention! [U83]
➤ **clueless** confused; ignorant | After the profes-sor spent three hours explaining the home-work, I was still clueless. | She is clueless about the plight of third world nations. [C75 college students: 'ignorant'; U83]

cobwebs see **have cobwebs**

coinkidink coincidence | What a coinkidink that we have two classes together. (pronounced [ko-íŋkidiŋk], like "co-" plus "in" plus "kid" plus "ink")

coke bottle eyes condition acquired when a person is intoxicated, in which all members of the opposite sex be-come appealing | Don't drink too much when we get to Biff's party because you'll get coke bottle eyes and maybe

COKE BOTTLE EYES

meet someone who isn't nice. [C77: coke-bottle glasses 'very thick eyeglass lenses'. See also **beer goggles.**]

cold chill to relax, take it easy, *kick back.* | —What did you do last night? —We just cold chilled at my place.

comatose drunk, intoxicated

combo bisexual person

Come on! 1. Stop it! 2. *Be real!* | As I tickled Chris, he screamed, "Come on!" [C79: an exclamation of disbelief, disapproval, request, etc.]

come on to to make a pass at [C79: come on 'present oneself as'; come-on 'enticement']

come out moldy / come up moldy to be humiliated, *molded, moded* [See also **molded.**]

COME OUT
MOLDY

commander see **couch commander**

complete real, true, *total* | When I first saw my sister's boyfriend I thought he was a complete barney.

consume to drink an alcoholic beverage | Let's go to the party. I'm ready to consume.

control see **out of control**

< > marks words or usages that may be offensive to some or all speakers and that therefore should be used only with discretion; C = Chapman's *New Dictionary of American Slang*; U = previously collected UCLA slang. See the Introduction for more discussion. The Pronunciation Guide provides an explanation of the symbols used in phonetic transcriptions.

cook up with to make out with | I cooked up with her at the party.

COOK UP WITH

cookies see **blow chunks**

cool 1. very good, excellent, neat. 2. to relax, take it easy, *gel, kick back* (pronounced like standard "cool" or [kӯúl]—rhymes with "yule") | I went shopping yesterday and I saw a dress that was very cool. | I'm just cooling. Come on over. [(1) C81 beat & cool talk & counterculture; U83 ("old"), 84; U83: [kӯúl]; (2) C81: cool it 'relax'. See also **No Cool, So Cool, That's cool! uncool**]

cop some Zs see **catch some Zs**

copious a lot of | I've got copious homework.

corporate sophisticated-looking, businesslike, professional-looking | She just looks corporate. Every day she is so well groomed.

CORPORATE

cosmo *trendy,* in vogue, happening | Chinois on Main is the cosmo restaurant this year. [C83: 'cosmopolitanism']

couch commander 1. T.V. remote control. 2. person with the T.V. remote control

COUCH COMMANDER

couch potato very lazy person who usually just lies around [C84: 'habitual lounger, esp a person who spends much time watching television']

coyote ugly ugly (of a person—so ugly that if you were to find yourself waking up next to such a person after a beer goggles evening, and if he or she were sleeping on your arm, you would rather bite  COYOTE UGLY your own arm off to escape than wake him or her up) | I had a coyote ugly date.

crack to be very funny, to make people laugh | Joe, that joke you told was hysterical. You totally crack! [C85: 'go into hysteria. See also **be in (someone's) crack.**]

crack a fart to pass gas, fart | What's that smell? Did someone crack a fart? [C92: 'cut a fart']

crack the books /crack it to study | I have to head home so I can start cracking the books. [C85 students]

 CRACK A FART

crank on to work efficiently on, to do well on; to go fast on | I cranked on that test. (U87: 'work on at a highly efficient, intense pace']
➤ **cranking** fun, exciting | That party last night was so cranking. I had the best time.

crash to sleep | She was tired, so I let her crash in my room. [C87: 'to go to sleep'; U83]

creek see **up shit creek**

< > marks words or usages that may be offensive to some or all speakers and that therefore should be used only with discretion; C = Chapman's *New Dictionary of American Slang;* U = previously collected UCLA slang. See the Introduction for more discussion. The Pronunciation Guide provides an explanation of the symbols used in phonetic transcriptions.

creep to flirt, make out (usually with more than one person) | Steve was creeping at the party on Friday.

CREEP

crib see **the crib**

criminal see **fashion criminal**

C.R.S. forgetful; stupid | He's so C.R.S.! [<c̱an't ṟemember s̱hit]

cruise 1. to go around looking for action (a party or something else happening); to leave. 2. to fulfill one's obligations (in or out of class) with minimal effort | I'll be cruising around the neighborhood. [(1) C89: 'to drive slowly and watchfully in the streets, walk about vigilantly in bars and parties, etc., looking for a sex partner'; (2) C89: 'be smoothly going about one's business']

CRUISE

➤ **cruise in / cruise through** to fulfill one's obligations with minimal effort in | I'm cruising in chemistry. | I'm cruising through work.

crunchy / crunchy granola natural-looking, having a healthy life-style and diet, earthy | She's a crunchy granola girl. [See also **granola.**]

C.S.P. casual sex partner, person one sleeps with to whom one is not committed | After Paul had been here for four days in a row, we asked Tami if he and she were together. She replied, "No, he's just my C.S.P." [<c̱asual s̱ex p̱artner]

Cujo someone who does dangerous or risky things, someone who (usually unintentionally) puts others in danger | Oh no, Cujo is driving. He goes too fast around those sharp turns and cliffs. [<the Stephen King novel and movie]

CUJO

cut / cut up having well defined muscles, *ripped* | The guy we saw lifting weights at the gym is really cut up.

cut up 1. to act crazy. 2. to make (someone) laugh. 3. to criticize—often, behind (someone's) back | He was cutting up. [C93 middle 1800s: 'to behave frivolously']

➤ **cut-up** funny person [C93 esp late 1800s: 'entertaining person']

cuts see **give (someone) cuts, have cuts, take cuts**

Dd

da kine see **the kind**

daddy see **freak daddy**

dagger <homosexual female> [C50 fr black: bull-dagger. See also **throw the dagger.**]

dance see **do the deed**

< > marks words or usages that may be offensive to some or all speakers and that therefore should be used only with discretion; C = Chapman's *New Dictionary of American Slang;* U = previously collected UCLA slang. See the Introduction for more discussion. The Pronunciation Guide provides an explanation of the symbols used in phonetic transcriptions.

dank 1. bad. 2. very good, *awesome* | That movie was really dank. | Did you see that brand-new Corvette? What a dank car!

date see **P.P.D., prom date**

Dead Week the last week of school before finals | I'm surprised the Union doesn't run out of coffee during Dead Week.

deadhead hippie, person who is into nature | Cindy is a total deadhead. If she could draw flowers on her face, go barefoot, and wear jean cutoffs to work, she would. [<the Grateful Dead; ? C97: 'stupid person'; 'extremely boring person']

deadly 1. very good. 2. very bad | She had on the most deadly outfit; I totally loved it. | That calculus test was so deadly. I know I failed. [C97: 'boring'; 'excellent'; U84: 'great'. See also **do the deadly deed.**]

DEADLY

deal see **Good deal! What is the deal? What's the deal? What's the deal with**

decent very good, *cool*

deed see **do the deed, do the deadly deed**

def 1. really good, gorgeous. 2. very, definitely | She is really def! | He is def stupid. [<definitely]

demon from hell conniving, deceitful woman [<Sam Kinison song]

devirginize to be (someone's) first sexual partner; to give (someone) his or her first experience with something (smoking, drugs, etc.) [<de + virgin + ize]

dew see **knock the dew off the lily**

diabetes see **give (someone) cavities**

dick 1. to trick, deceive, be mean or unfair to, *screw over*. 2. jerk, mean person, offensive person; idiot (usually refers to a male) | The professor totally dicked me—he won't let me make up the midterm I missed because I had mono. | Jack is such a dick. When I asked him what the homework assignment was, he refused to tell me. [(1) C100: 'to potter or meddle'; (2) C101: 'despised person']
➤ **dick over** to trick, deceive

dickhead jerk | She's such a dickhead —she only cares about herself. [C101: 'despised person']

DICKHEAD

dicktease woman who acts as if she likes a man, but then turns him down or becomes cold to him when he asks her out | That dicktease won't even speak to me today. I don't get it! [See also **pricktease**.]

dickweed / dickwad jerk, idiot, *asshole* | That guy is a total dickwad. He took two parking spaces.

Did you get any pieces? Did you *score*? Did you

< > marks words or usages that may be offensive to some or all speakers and that therefore should be used only with discretion; C = Chapman's *New Dictionary of American Slang*; U = previously collected UCLA slang. See the Introduction for more discussion. The Pronunciation Guide provides an explanation of the symbols used in phonetic transcriptions.

have sex with anyone? [C322: piece 'the sex act'. See also **get a piece of.**]

die to have a hard time; to be upset | I was dying on that test—I had to guess on over half the questions! [U84: dying 'having a hard time'. See also **Surf or die! Thrash or die!**]

DIE

diem see **Carpe diem!**

dig to understand [C101 cool talk & counterculture, fr jive talk; U83: You dig? 'Do you understand?']

➤ **dig / dig on** to like | I dig that shirt—it looks cool on you. [C101 cool talk & counterculture, fr jive talk]

dimbo very stupid, *airheaded* girl, a dumb bimbo | That dimbo probably couldn't find her way home from her own backyard. [<dumb bimbo / dim bimbo]

DIMBO

ding 1. to break up with, drop. 2. to refuse membership or drop from membership (a potential or active member—fraternity term) | He dinged her after they had been dating for six months. [C102 college students: 'to vote against a candidate for membership; blackball']

dingleberry little piece of fecal matter (for instance, floating in the toilet after it has been flushed, or sticking to anal hair)

dis / diss 1. to be mean or disrespectful toward,

to embarrass, put down, *cap on.* 2. to do wrong to, ignore, *dog, blow off.* 3. disappointment, *burn, bummer* | The teacher always calls on me when he knows I don't know the answer. I swear he's always dissing me. | That C− on my paper was a total dis. [<the prefix dis-, as in dis<u>re</u>spect, <u>dis</u>regard, <u>dis</u>appointment, etc.)]

DIS

dismiss to break up with | I dismissed Eric—now he's history.

diss see **dis**

ditch see **be in the ditch**

ditz a *ditzy* person, an *airhead* [C105]
➤ **ditzy** flighty, dingy, *airheaded*

do 1. hairdo, hairstyle. 2. to have sex with | I got my do whacked yesterday. Do you like it? | Look at her do, it's to the curb. | He did her. | She did him. [(1) <hair<u>do</u>; C106 esp black; (2) C108: do it]

DITZ

do a beer bong to drink beer through a beer bong

do a fruit salad to expose one's genitals in a socially unacceptable context (of a male)

do oneself to bring embarrassment to oneself | I can't believe you are going to tell that story—don't do yourself.

< > marks words or usages that may be offensive to some or all speakers and that therefore should be used only with discretion; C = Chapman's *New Dictionary of American Slang;* U = previously collected UCLA slang. See the Introduction for more discussion. The Pronunciation Guide provides an explanation of the symbols used in phonetic transcriptions.

do righteous 1. to do good. 2. to do good to | Tom dealt me a good hand. He really did me righteous. [C359 black, fr 1930s jazz musicians: righteous 'excellent']
➤ **do righteous by** to do good to | Do righteous by me!

do the deed / do the do / do the bone dance / do the nasty / do the wild thing to have sex | They did the do in his back seat. | My parents walked in while I was doing the bone dance and grounded me until I was forty. | Sheila couldn't go home on Monday 'cause her roommate was doing the wild thing with her boyfriend. [C108: do it. See also **the wild thing.**]
➤ **do the deadly deed** to have sex without a condom

do up to do something to | When I saw that evil look in his eye, I knew he was going to try to do me up. [C112: 'to pummel and trounce']
➤ **do up with** to give (something) to | He did me up with some drugs.

Do you see skid marks on my forehead? Do I seem that stupid? [U84]

doctor alcoholic beverage | Hand me the doctor. [See also **go to the doctor.**]

dode unappealing person, stupid person, idiot, *dork, barney* | What a dode; his pants are four inches too short. [?<u>dork</u> + <u>dude</u>]

dog 1. to do wrong; to fail to keep an appointment with, *flake on*; to lie, avoid giving information to; to stare at, give a dirty look to; to ignore; *dis, blow off.* 2. person who does wrong to someone else. 3. disappointment, *burn, bummer, diss.* | That guy just flipped me off. It was the ultimate dog. [C107 Army: 'to pester'; esp black: 'untrustworthy man, seducer'; U84: 'to ignore']

➤ **dog on** to talk badly about, criticize, *bag on, rag on*; to lead on | We dogged on him (talked badly about him). | She dogged him on (led him on).

dolled out dolled up, dressed up

dolomite cocaine

dong see **cheese dong**

DOLLED OUT

donor person who makes himself or herself available for sexual intercourse

Don't you hate it when that happens? (comment on a situation in which one is made aware of an unfortunate but rare occurrence) | John just told me the elevators in his office building were out of order and he had to climb thirty-two flights of stairs. Don't you hate it when that happens? [<"Saturday Night Live"]

doobage marijuana

< > marks words or usages that may be offensive to some or all speakers and that therefore should be used only with discretion; C = Chapman's *New Dictionary of American Slang*; U = previously collected UCLA slang. See the Introduction for more discussion. The Pronunciation Guide provides an explanation of the symbols used in phonetic transcriptions.

➤ **doobie** joint, marijuana cigarette | We'd better roll some doobies before we go to the Grateful Dead concert.

doofus *geek,* stupid person, person lacking social skills (pronounced [dúfəs], like "doo-fuss") | Oh my God, I'm such a doofus! I can't believe I just spilled all over you! [C118: dufus 'stupid, blundering'; U84: duffus / duhface]

DOOFUS

dooie 1. pow (the sound of a punch or slap). 2. to punch, beat up (pronounced [dúwi], like "Dewey") | That guy really made me angry, so I beat him up. Dooie, dooie, dooie. | He still wouldn't shut up so I dooied him again.

door see **penny a door**

dork 1. stupid person, idiot. 2. to have sex with [C110: dork 'despicable person')

➤ **dork off** to fool around, to mess around, to not do as one is told

➤ **dorkmunder** stupid person, idiot | My lab partner's a total dorkmunder.

➤ **dorky** stupid, idiotic; ugly [C110: 'stupid, awkward'; U87: 'ugly']

dorm rat / dorm frog student who lives in the dorms for more than a year or who rarely leaves the dorms

double bagger see **two bagger**

doubt see **No doubt!**

doughhead idiot | That guy in my Management class always gets lost on his way to class—what a doughhead. [C112]

DOUGHHEAD

down 1. to drink down, finish drinking. 2. to beat up | He downed a beer. | Did you see the shiner on Sam? His girlfriend must have downed him again. [C112: 'to eat or drink'. See also **get busy, Take it down a thousand!**]

drag tiresome or annoying person or thing | It's such a drag to go and buy rats for my snake to eat every week. [C112 middle 1800s; U83]

DRAG

➤ **drag down** to depress, upset | He really drags me down.

dragging see **be dragging**

dragon 1. penis. 2. person with bad breath. | I hate having class with Mark—he's such a dragon. [See also **drain the dragon.**]

drain the dragon / drain the main vein to urinate (of a man) | He was draining the main vein on a tree!

dream see **pirate's dream**

drive the bus / drive the porcelain bus to vomit into the toilet | —Where's Frank? —He's in the john driving the bus. He had too much to drink.

< > marks words or usages that may be offensive to some or all speakers and that therefore should be used only with discretion; C = Chapman's *New Dictionary of American Slang;* U = previously collected UCLA slang. See the Introduction for more discussion. The Pronunciation Guide provides an explanation of the symbols used in phonetic transcriptions.

[C115: drive the big bus 'vomit into the toilet, especially from drunkenness']

drought see **be in a drought, bootie drought**

duck unappealing person, misfit, *nerd, geek* | Randy is totally uncool. He's such a duck. [C118 middle 1800s: 'man, fellow'. See also **Fuck a duck!**]

dud see **good dud**

dude 1. person, guy. 2. (term of address) | That guy is just the coolest person. He is a jamming dude. | Hey, dude, what's up? [C118 esp black: 'man, fellow']

➤ **Dude!** Hey! Wow! Gee! Shit!

➤ **Dude man!** What's up?

<**dumbfuck**> stupid person, *geek*

dunt person who could be mistaken for someone of the opposite sex | We all screamed when Karen walked into the locker room—she's a real dunt. [<u>d</u>ick + c<u>unt</u>]

DUNT

dupe to do wrong to | My ride left me at the game; he fully duped me.

dust to insult, humiliate, *burn* [See also **be dust.**]

➤ **dusted** insulted, humiliated, *burned* | He was dusted when his girlfriend proved him wrong.

➤ **dusty** having a bad attitude | Christin is dusty today; I wonder why.

dweeb fool, idiot [C120 teenagers: 'despised person'; U87]

dyno pretty; excellent | That chick is dyno. | Marcie, that dinner you made was way dyno. [C188: dynamite, dy-no-mite]

E e

earl to vomit | She earled all over the carpet.

Easy! / Easy, tiger! / Easy, sober! / Easy, champ! Calm down! | Easy, tiger! You'll get your chance to refute his argument in a minute. [See also **Take it easy!**]

EASY!

<**Eat me!**> Shut up! You make me sick! Get out of here! Kiss my ass! *Fuck you!* [C122: eat it (an exclamation of contempt and defiance)]

eddie ugly guy

eggo idiot, socially outdated person, *nerd* | Rob is such an eggo. He wears bell-bottoms and platforms.

eighty-six to get rid of | The teacher lets us eighty-six our lowest score. [C123: 'kill, destroy']

Einstein pubic hair | You could see part of her Einstein sticking out of her bikini.

even see **not even, Odd or Even**

eye see **the fuck eye**

< > marks words or usages that may be offensive to some or all speakers and that therefore should be used only with discretion; C = Chapman's *New Dictionary of American Slang;* U = previously collected UCLA slang. See the Introduction for more discussion. The Pronunciation Guide provides an explanation of the symbols used in phonetic transcriptions.

eye boogers small clumps of eye mucus [C49: booger 'piece of solid mucus from the nose']

eyes breasts | She's got some big eyes. [See also **coke bottle eyes, fuck-me eyes, hands.**]

F f

F! (an exclamation of extreme disappointment or pain) | F! I just bombed that test! [<Fuck!]

face insult, burn | What a face! [? <have a red face, get egg on one's face. See also **be in (someone's) face, fuckface, Get out of my face! pizza face**]

FACE

➤ **Face!** *Burn!* (exclamation used after an insult or burn)

➤ **faced** totally outdone; embarrassed [U83, 87. See also **shitfaced.**]

__-factor__ quantity of (noun) | The squeeze-factor in that game was awfully high. | The skank-factor at the party was good.

fade to get tired | I am fading. I should probably go to bed really soon. [C127: 'to lose power and effectiveness']

fag see **art fag, frat dick**

<**fag hag**> girl who has many male homosexual friends | Whenever I see Mary she's always hanging

out with one of her gay friends. She's such a fag hag.

fail to not understand or comprehend | The teacher just went off on a complete tangent. I fail.

fake-bake 1. tanning salon. 2. to go to a tanning salon. 3. fake tan | When girls have tan legs in the middle of February, you can tell they totally fake-bake. | Look at Tiffany's fake-bake!

FAKE-BAKE

False! No way! You're exaggerating! You're lying! | —I was so thirsty this morning I drank a whole gallon of milk. —False!

fan to skip | Let's fan chemistry. I'd rather hit the beach.

fart see **Brainfart! crack a fart**

fartsy see **artsy**

fashion arrest see **make a fashion arrest**

fashion criminal / fashion mutant person who tries unsuccessfully to make individualistic fashion statements

fashion police imaginary authoritative body responsible for finding and arresting people who dress unfashionably | Look at that hideous outfit! Someone call the fashion police!

FASHION POLICE

< > marks words or usages that may be offensive to some or all speakers and that therefore should be used only with discretion; C = Chapman's *New Dictionary of American Slang*; U = previously collected UCLA slang. See the Introduction for more discussion. The Pronunciation Guide provides an explanation of the symbols used in phonetic transcriptions.

fashion risk ugly item of clothing | That shirt is a fashion risk. [See also **take a fashion risk.**]

fashion victim person who wears clothes that don't look right: especially, person who wears trendy clothes without regard to what looks good on him or her; slave to fashion

FASHION VICTIM

fast see **so fast**

favors see **party favors**

Fear! How scary! | She's going out with Mark again? Fear!

feel moldy to feel humiliated

<**fembo**> homosexual man

FEAR!

__**-fest** abundance of (noun) | I just got back from the beach. What a skinfest! [C132 late 1800s]

fifi superficial-looking girl with a trendy style of dress; for instance, one who has bleached, teased blond hair, a Day-Glo spandex skirt, and a skin-tight top showing her stomach

filet girl, cute girl | In her video "Touch Me" Samantha Fox is a filet. (pronounced [fυlé], like "fill" plus "A")

FIFI

find a clue see **get a clue**

fine extremely attractive, good looking | Todd, look

at her! She is fine! | Joe, your new girlfriend is fine; she's got blond hair, blue eyes, and the sexiest legs I've ever seen.

fire see **Hell's bells!**

fire on to reprimand, argue with, tell off, *rip on* | She fired on me for being late. [C134 black: 'strike, hit']

fire up to get excited, to be happy, to be dedicated | We really have to fire up for this event if it is going to be a successful fund-raiser. [C134: fire someone up 'to fill someone with energy and enthusiasm, excite someone'. See also **on fire.**]

FIRE UP

➤ **fired up** excited | We were all fired up for the big game this weekend. | I am totally fired up over my A on my midterm. [C134]

fish see **chum the fish**

five miles of bad road see **like five miles of bad road**

fix see **hormone fix**

flack see **catch flack, give (someone) flack**

flag to fail | I'm going to go flag my finals.

flail 1. to get a failing grade because of being flustered. 2. to fail (a test) because of being flustered [<fluster + fail]

< > marks words or usages that may be offensive to some or all speakers and that therefore should be used only with discretion; C = Chapman's *New Dictionary of American Slang;* U = previously collected UCLA slang. See the Introduction for more discussion. The Pronunciation Guide provides an explanation of the symbols used in phonetic transcriptions.

flake 1. to fail to keep an appointment or commitment. 2. irresponsible person, person who flakes on others, *airhead, ditz* | I was expecting Mike to arrive at six o'clock, and since it's already seven o'clock, I guess he flaked. | This is the third time you've canceled on me. You're such a flake! [C137 teenagers: flake off 'to leave'; jazz musicians: flake out 'leave'; teenagers: 'stupid, erratic person'; U84: 'unreliable person']

➤ **flake major** major that has the reputation of being easy (or easy to get into) or not applicable to one's future life

➤ **flake on** to fail to keep an appointment with or commitment to | Brian was supposed to meet me here for dinner over half an hour ago, but it looks like he's flaked on me. [U87]

➤ **flaky** disorganized, flighty, fickle, unreliable [C137 baseball: 'colorfully eccentric'; 'insane'; 'disoriented'; U84: flakey 'unreliable']

flame <to appear blatantly homosexual (of a man)> | All the guys outside that bar really flame. [C137]

➤ **flamer / flame** <blatantly homosexual man> [C137]

➤ **flaming** <blatantly homosexual> [C137]

FLAME

Fletch see **pull a Fletch**

flick off see **flip off**

flip / flip out to get excited; to be surprised,

shocked, disbelieving | You will flip out when you hear the news I have about Mark and Carrie. [C140: 'to display enthusiasm'; 'to go insane']

flip a bitch to make an illegal U-turn | When Mark saw that no traffic was coming, he flipped a bitch in the middle of the street instead of waiting until the next intersection.

flip off / flick off to make an obscene gesture at (someone) by sticking out one's middle finger while leaving the others in a fist [See also **give (some-one) the bird.**]

flip out see **flip**

flip (somone) the bone see **give (someone) the bird**

Flo see Aunt Flo

fluff to pass gas, fart | After he fluffed, everyone left the room.

flute see **play the skin flute**

fly stylish, attractive, excellent, *cool* [C142 esp black fr early 1900s: 'stylish, very attractive'. See also **keg fly.**]
➤ **fly girl** *cool* girl
➤ **fly guy** *cool* guy

FLUFF

Flynn see **in like Flynn**

< > marks words or usages that may be offensive to some or all speakers and that therefore should be used only with discretion; C = Chapman's *New Dictionary of American Slang;* U = previously collected UCLA slang. See the Introduction for more discussion. The Pronunciation Guide provides an explanation of the symbols used in phonetic transcriptions.

F.O.! Get out of here! You make me sick! Stay away from me! | I don't want to see your slimy face any more. Just F.O! [<<u>F</u>uck <u>o</u>ff]

fold to become tired | Don't fold! The second feature starts in ten minutes! It's only two A.M.! [C143: 'lose effect and energy, wilt, fade']

➤ **folder** one who is always tired early in the evening | Don't ask her to go out with us tonight—she's a folder.

foof superficial person, very artificial person | So she goes, "Where's my hairspray? I need hairspray!" What a total foof! [? C143: foofooraw 'ostentation']

forehead see **Do you see skid marks on my forehead?**

fossil person who has been a college student for more than four years | My G.E. course is just filled with fossils that are trying to finish their requirements so they can graduate this year. [C145: 'old person']

FOSSIL

foul see **party foul**

frat boy / frat brat see **frat rat**

frat dick / <frat fag> member of a fraternity who drinks a lot, womanizes, and has an elitist attitude about his fraternity | Mark is a total frat dick. I haven't seen him in class or without a beer in his hand for years.

---

frat rat / frat brat / frat boy / fraternity boy
member of a fraternity | All of the frat rats swarmed
around the table. [C146: frat rat]

freak 1. attractive girl. 2. weird-looking
girl, slut. 3. to dance very seductively |
—Wow, that chick's a freak! —Yeah, she's
hot. [U84: freakozoid 'mate so perfect he/she
must have been created for one'. See also
freak out.]

FREAK

➤ **freak daddy** cute male, *babe, studmuffin*
➤ **freak mama** 1. attractive slut. 2. cute female,
babe, studmuffin [C272 black: mama 'sexually
attractive or sexually available woman']
➤ **freak on / freak all over** to dance very seduc-
tively with | The ho at the nightclub was freak-
ing all over some guy.

freak out / freak 1. to become overwhelmed by
surprise, nervousness, or anxiety. 2. to surprise,
scare | On "Days of Our Lives," Roman freaked out
when he discovered that Marlena hadn't died in a
plane crash two years ago. | Barbara is going to
freak when I tell her she got an F on the test that
she studied for. [C147: 'go out of touch with reality
. . . become irrational'; 'become very excited and ex-
hilarated'; U83]

fred 1. to vomit. 2. socially unacceptable person,
freeloader, idiot, jerk, stupid person, klutz, *geek* |

< > marks words or usages that may be offensive to some or all speakers and that therefore
should be used only with discretion; C = Chapman's *New Dictionary of American Slang*; U =
previously collected UCLA slang. See the Introduction for more discussion. The Pronunciation
Guide provides an explanation of the symbols used in phonetic transcriptions.

When Mark missed an easy shot during a basket-ball game his teammates called him a fred. [<Fred, a character in "The Flintstones"]

fresh very good or exciting; attractive, stylish | It was the freshest ball game I have ever played—we won fifteen to four! [C148: 'aloof and uninvolved, cool'. See also **bust fresh.**]

fried 1. drunk, intoxicated. 2. sunburned | She was so fried that no one would let her drive home. [C148]

frito toes smelly feet | When Bill came home from work, he took off his shoes. We said, "Get those frito toes out of here."

FRITO TOES

frog see **dorm rat**

from hell of an extremely bad type | And then he lost his wallet. It was just a date from hell.

front see **try to front**

froyo frozen yogurt | Let's get some froyo. They're having a two-for-one at Baskin-Robbins. [<frozen yogurt]

fruit salad see **do a fruit salad**

<**fuck**> idiot, jerk [C151. See also **Bumblefuck, dumbfuck, mindfuck, ratfuck, the fuck, the fuck eye, What the hell?!**]

fuck eyes see **fuck-me eyes**

<Fuck me!> Damn! Shut up! You make me sick! Get out of here! Kiss my ass! I'm *screwed*!

➤ **<Fuck a duck!>** Damn! [C151]

➤ **<Fuck me hard!>** Damn! Shit! Get out of here! I'm *screwed*!

➤ **<Fuck that noise!>** Forget it! What a drag! *Bullshit!*

<Fuck you!> I don't believe you! Be quiet! You're wrong! | You're going to fly your own plane to London? Fuck you! | Fuck you! Don't tell me what to do! | Fuck you! I did not go out with Dave last night! [C152: (an exclamation of very strong defiance and contempt)]

<fuck up> to make a mistake, do badly [C152]

➤ **<fuck with>** to mess with, bother, deceive, *screw over* [C152]

FUCK WITH

➤ **<fucked, fucked up>** 1. drunk, intoxicated; under the influence of drugs. 2. in a bad situation, messed up, negatively affected. 3. absentminded, unfair, jerky | I was fucked up after having twelve beers. [C151: fucked up. See also **mindfucked.**]

<fuckface, fuckhead> *asshole* [C151: fuckhead 'despicable person']

<fucking> 1. incredibly, very, totally, completely.

<> marks words or usages that may be offensive to some or all speakers and that therefore should be used only with discretion; C = Chapman's *New Dictionary of American Slang;* U = previously collected UCLA slang. See the Introduction for more discussion. The Pronunciation Guide provides an explanation of the symbols used in phonetic transcriptions.

2. damn, damned. 3. um (word used when hesitating or unsure how to continue) | We had a fucking good time at the party. | And then after that, let's see, fucking . . . I went to the movies, and . . . [(1, 2) C151. See also **A.S.A.F.P., T.F.A.**]

➤ <**Fucking A!**> Wow! Damn! Oh! Cool! Oh, shit! [?<<u>a</u>ss; C151]

<**fuck-me boots**> midcalf or higher boots worn with a miniskirt [See also **C.F.M.**]

<**fuck-me eyes**> / <**fuck eyes**> flirtatious stares or glances | I'm feeling some serious fuck-me eyes from that guy in the corner. [<the movie *Cocktail*. See also **the fuck eye.**]

FUCK-ME BOOTS

<**fuckstrated**> sexually frustrated | Biff broke up with his girlfriend and hasn't had sex in three weeks; he's so fuckstrated. [<<u>fuck</u> + frus<u>trated</u>]

FUCKSTRATED

<**fuck-up**> obnoxious person, person who does nothing right, gets in the way, or is unmotivated, *loser* [<fuck up; C152: 'bungler']

fugly very ugly | She's so fugly she makes my mother-in-law look cute. [<<u>fu</u>cking <u>ugly</u>. See also **mufugly.**]

full-on / full complete and total, absolute | My roommate's half of the room is ankle-deep in dirty clothes; he's a full-on slob. | That betty over there is the full babe. [U83: full-on 'very, totally']

fully totally, really | I fully didn't expect to get an A on that test.

fumunda cheese smegma (pronounced [fəmʌndə], like "fum" plus "un" plus "duh") [<from under]

funky bizarre; fashionably eccentric, slightly unfashionable yet still accept-able | Genie, those purple shoes are funky, but I like them. [C153: 'ex-cellent, effective'; 'old-fashioned, quaintly out-of-date'; 'pleasantly eccentric'; U84]

FUNKY

future see **Good future!**

fuzz see **bump fuzz**

<**fuzz bumper**> female homosexual

Gg

gaff to insult, ignore, skip, *blow off* | He to-tally gaffed her. | I gaffed my dentist ap-pointment today. [? C155: 'cheat']

gagger disgusting person or thing | That geek is such a gagger. [<gag + er]

GAGGER

< > marks words or usages that may be offensive to some or all speakers and that therefore should be used only with discretion; C = Chapman's *New Dictionary of American Slang;* U = previously collected UCLA slang. See the Introduction for more discussion. The Pronunciation Guide provides an explanation of the symbols used in phonetic transcriptions.

gal see **Yah, gal, what is?**

ganja marijuana (pronounced [gánjə], with first syllable like "gone") | Last night we all smoked some ganja. [C156: 'strong type of marijuana obtained from a cultivated strain of Indian hemp']

<**gash**> to have sex | We gashed. [C157: 'the sex act']

gay stupid; ugly; corny, weird | The clarinet player looked totally gay in his band uniform. | I would never buy that sweater, it's gay. | Harry ran into class ten minutes late and handed our T.A.

GAY

an apple. He's so gay. [C157 homosexuals, 1930s or earlier: 'homosexual'; U84: 'weird, strange, different'. See also **homosexual, queer.**]

G.D.I. person who is not a member of a fraternity or sorority | Who says you have to be a frat rat to party hearty? Half the school was raging at my place Friday night, and I'm a G.D.I.! [<god-damned independent]

gears see **reverse gears**

geeba marijuana | I don't buy geeba, I grow it. (pronounced [jíbə], like "gee" plus "buh")

geek stupid person, idiot, *dork, nerd;* unusual person [C159: 'pervert or degenerate'; U83, 84]
➤ **Geek** Greek; sorority or fraternity member

gel to relax, kick back | After having five hours of class today I think I'll go home and gel. [U83: 'participate in activities of little value'; 84: 'make a mistake']

GEL

➤ **gel on** to fail to keep an appointment with, to *flake on*

get a C.B. see **have a C.B.**

get a clue / find a clue to think sensibly; not to be so stupid, naive, or ignorant (*got a clue, *getting a clue, *found a clue, *finding a clue) | My friend told me to get a clue about the assignment because she couldn't spend all night explaining it to me. [C159 teenagers: 'to understand, grasp'; U83, 84. See also **clueless, have a clue.**]

GET A CLUE

Get a job! Find something to do with yourself!

Get a life! Do something constructive with your time! Stop being such a jerk! Mind your own business! Improve your social life! Have some ambition! | Geez, Joe, you're a twenty-seven-year-old burger fryer at Big Tommie's. Get a life! [See also **have no life.**]

get a piece of / have a piece of <to have sex with (a woman)> | Julie is a total skeezer. I would

< > marks words or usages that may be offensive to some or all speakers and that therefore should be used only with discretion; C = Chapman's *New Dictionary of American Slang;* U = previously collected UCLA slang. See the Introduction for more discussion. The Pronunciation Guide provides an explanation of the symbols used in phonetic transcriptions.

love to get a piece of her. [See also **Did you get any pieces?**]

get busy / get down to have sex | Let's get busy. [C160 teenagers: get down 'enjoy oneself, have fun'; U83]

GET BUSY

get flack see **catch flack**

get iced to get stood up, get let down [C223: ice 'ignore someone, snub'; U87]

get in (someone's) face to confront, provoke, bother (someone) [C161; U87]

get loose 1. to throw punches. 2. to dance, to have fun. 3. to become intensely involved
➤ **get loose on** to throw punches at, to yell at

GET LOOSE

get off to stop bothering, get away from | Get off me big time. I'm gonna score. [C161: get off someone's back; C162: 'get off someone's case']
➤ **get off on** 1. to be excited by. 2. to insult, to bag on. 3. to get angry at | I got off on Jane after she called me stupid. [C162: 'enjoy greatly']

Get out of here! Shut up! You're lying! Get serious!

Get out of my face! Stop bothering me! [C162]

get raked see **be raked**

Get real! see **Be real!**

get sloppy 1. to have sex. 2. to get drunk

get some / have some to make out, have sex, *score* | Everyone told me my date was a strawberry, so I fully expected to get some, but she turned out to be a total prude. [See also **get a piece of, get some trim, want some.**]

GET SLOPPY

➤ **get some scrumptious** to make out with someone (usually used by females)

➤ **get some trim** to have sex (of a male) [C446 black: 'the sex act with a woman'. See also **get some.**]

get together to make out; to have sex | Oh, you wouldn't believe who I met last night. . . . and we got together. . . . of course he was a good kisser.

ghost person who rarely comes around or shows up | Ever since he met his new girlfriend, John has been a total ghost.

giant see **mental giant**

gig 1. to have a one-night stand. 2. to leave | Stu has an awesome body, I just want to gig with him. [C164 musicians fr 1930s: 'a playing date or engagement, esp a one-night job']

GHOST

<**gimp**> coward, weakling, *loser, geek* | That guy is a total gimp. He isn't strong enough to even hold the football, let alone play the game. [C165]

< > marks words or usages that may be offensive to some or all speakers and that therefore should be used only with discretion; C = Chapman's *New Dictionary of American Slang;* U = previously collected UCLA slang. See the Introduction for more discussion. The Pronunciation Guide provides an explanation of the symbols used in phonetic transcriptions.

girl see **fly girl, homegirl**

give attitude / give tude see **throw attitude**

give (someone) a melvin to yank (someone's) underwear up abruptly or roughly [See also **have a melvin.**]

give (someone) a perm to perform oral sex on (someone), give (someone) a blow job

GIVE (SOMEONE) A PERM

give (someone) cavities / give (someone) diabetes to be nauseatingly sweet to (someone) | She was so sweet she gave people cavities when she smiled.

give (someone) cuts to let (someone) into a line [See also **have cuts, take cuts.**]

give (someone) flack to give (someone) negative verbal feedback | She gave me a lot of flack when I told her she was wrong. [C137: flak, flack 'severe criticism']

GIVE (SOMEONE) FLACK

give (someone) hemorrhoids to bother (someone) | He gives me hemorrhoids. [See also **hemorrhoid.**]

give (someone) the bird / give (someone) the bone / flip (someone) the bone to make an obscene gesture at (someone) by sticking out one's middle finger while leaving the others in a fist | Do you have to give the bone to everyone who cuts you off? [C167: give someone the finger; 140: flip the bird; U87. See also **flip off.**]

give (someone) the hot beef injection see **slip (someone) the hot beef injection**

globes breasts | Nice globes, babe! [C168]

glued sane, psychologically stable | You are such a good friend—I'd go crazy without you here to keep me glued. [C79: come unglued 'go out of control']

GLOBES

gnarly 1. awful, far-out, scary, mind-blowing, *hairy*. 2. *cool* | That girl is gnarly. She goes to every party there is. [C169 teenagers: 'excellent, wonderful': U83: 'awful'; 83: 'good'; 84: 'wonderful']

go to say (mainly used in telling a story) | And then he goes, "I've been busy all day." And then I go, "Well, I just felt like an old chair waiting for you to call." [C169 teenagers esp fr late 1960s: 'to say'; U83]

go aggro to get wild, become aggressive, do weird things | Dude, don't go aggro on me. [See also **aggro.**]

go balls out to put out all one's effort

➤ **go balls out on** to put all one's effort into | I went balls out on my paper. I finished it five minutes before it was due. [See also **Balls out!**]

< > marks words or usages that may be offensive to some or all speakers and that therefore should be used only with discretion; C = Chapman's *New Dictionary of American Slang;* U = previously collected UCLA slang. See the Introduction for more discussion. The Pronunciation Guide provides an explanation of the symbols used in phonetic transcriptions.

go for it to take a chance, to go ahead and try it [C171; U84]

go off 1. to become crazy or silly; to lose one's temper; to be intense (of a person). 2. to move from topic to topic in conversation | When he gets drunk, he totally goes off. | I couldn't follow the teacher when she went off.

GO OFF

go on a __ run to go to (noun), to go for (noun) | I'm going on a library run, so I won't be back for a while. | The party was going dry, so we had to go on a beer run.

go to the doctor / go to see the doctor / have a doctor's appointment to drink alcoholic beverages | I went to see the doctor last night.

go window shopping see **window shop**

god gorgeous guy | What a god! He is the cutest guy I have ever seen. [See also **bow to the porcelain god, hug the porcelain god, pray to the porcelain god, worship the porcelain god.**]

goddess female achiever, *stud, cool* person | You goddess! I can't believe that you did all the work I gave you in only two days. [See also **bow to the porcelain god, hug the porcelain god, make love to the porcelain goddess, pray to the porcelain god, worship the porcelain god.**]

GODDESS

➤ __ **goddess** female who does very well at (noun) or who (verb)'s very well | study goddess | soccer goddess

goggles see **beer goggles**

golden see **be golden**

gone 1. totally drunk, *wasted.* 2. crazy, *spaced out* | After drinking a twelve-pack, she was so gone. [C172 jazz musicians: 'intoxicated, esp with narcotics'; cool talk: "in a trancelike condition']

GONE

gonus stupid person, *dork* (pronounced [gónəs], like "go" plus a rhyme for "bus")

goob / goober person who exhibits strange or silly behavior, *loser* | I can't believe I used to go out with Greg. He is such a goober. [C173 teenagers: 'stupid and bizarre person']

good see **be up to no good, have a good personality**

Good deal! Right on! All right! | You got enrolled in all the classes you wanted? Good deal! [C173]

good dud unamusing joke | After Karen told me another knock-knock joke, I let her know it was a good dud. [C118 middle 1800s: dud 'failure']

GOOD DUD

< > marks words or usages that may be offensive to some or all speakers and that therefore should be used only with discretion; C = Chapman's *New Dictionary of American Slang;* U = previously collected UCLA slang. See the Introduction for more discussion. The Pronunciation Guide provides an explanation of the symbols used in phonetic transcriptions.

Good future! What a bad job! | You're a cashier at Big Burger? Good future! [U84]

gork *nerd, loser* | Hubert is such a gork. His glasses are always falling off his nose, and he wears plaids with stripes. [<u>g</u>eek + <u>dork</u>; C177 hospital: 'stuporous or imbecilic patient', <<u>G</u>od <u>o</u>nly <u>r</u>eally <u>k</u>nows]

goth / gothic 1. looking like a gothic: wearing black clothes, silver jewelry, pointed shoes, black lipstick, and so on. 2. person into Death Rock who dresses in gothic style

gouge to take something from, to cheat out of something; to insult, *screw over* | Jon has been hitting on Cindy all night, and Robert just gouged him by taking Cindy home.
➤ **Gouge!** (exclamation used after an insult)

G.Q. stylish, good-looking (of a male) | A guy who is G.Q. will usually make you swoon. [<*Gentleman's Quarterly;* U83, 84. See also **jeek.**]

grab to make out [C179: grab-ass 'sexual touching and clutching']
➤ **grab on** to make out with | They grabbed on each other.

GRAB

grader see **seventh grader**

grades see **AIDS for Grades**

granola natural-looking person (for instance, a girl who doesn't wear makeup) with a healthy life-style and diet | Stephanie turned into a granola when she started college. She won't even eat at McDonald's. [See also **crunchy.**]

grayhaired <old person> | There was a pack of grayhaireds in front of us on the stairs and we couldn't get by. [See also **bluehaired.**]

grease to make out | Last night I saw Bill again. . . . Yes, we greased again.

Greek member of a sorority or fraternity [C181 college students: 'college fraternity member']

grind 1. to eat. 2. to eat something, have some food. 3. to study. <4. to have wild sex.> 5. to move one's pelvis while dancing or making out (past: grinded) | I'm really hungry; let's go to McDonald's and grind. | I grinded all night for my biology midterm; I better nail that test. [C182 middle 1800s: 'to rotate one's pelvis . . .'; 'to study diligently'; U84: 'eat an outrageous amount' (past: grinded)]

GRIND

➤ **grinds** food, things to eat | Dude, these two chicks came over last night and made us the killer grinds.

grommet inexperienced little kid who annoys people by skateboarding on the sidewalk

GROMMET

groovy *cool*, neat, good | That man in

< > marks words or usages that may be offensive to some or all speakers and that therefore should be used only with discretion; C = Chapman's *New Dictionary of American Slang*; U = previously collected UCLA slang. See the Introduction for more discussion. The Pronunciation Guide provides an explanation of the symbols used in phonetic transcriptions.

the blue has on a groovy hat. [C183; U83: 'great'; 84: 'unattractive'; 87: 'outdated']

grossola see ___-ola

grovel to make out, neck, fool around (usually with someone who's not a regular date) | Singles bars are a great place to grovel. [U83, 87]

grub 1. to eat, have some food. 2. food, meal | Let's go grub now. [C184 late 1800s cowboys: 'food'; black (v)]

➤   **grub on** to eat (something) | When you called last night I was grubbing on some pizza.

gunner see **tail gunner**

guns biceps | He has really big guns.

guy male *nerd* | John is such a guy—just look at that calculator in his shirt pocket.   GUNS [C187 late 1800s: 'person of either sex, man, fellow'. See also **fly guy, N.G.B., SNAG.**]

Hh

ha see **brewhaha**

hag see **fag hag**

haha see **brewhaha**

hair see **big hair**

hairball person who gets drunk and acts completely raucous, rowdy, and obnoxious (often breaking things); *asshole,* jerk | Jon was being a hairball last night: he got heated and thrashed the whole upstairs—he broke out all the windows.

HAIRBALL

hairy weird, scary, complicated, *intense* [C190: 'difficult'; esp teenagers fr 1960s: 'frighteningly dangerous, hair-raising, scary']

half see **a__ and a half**

hammer to drink rapidly (usually a beer) | Paul hammered three beers as soon as he got home from school.

➤ **hammered** drunk, intoxicated | God, my hangover is so bad. I was totally hammered last night. [C191; U87]

handle to deal with pressure; to accept or tolerate a situation | This class is so boring I can't handle. [See also **hang.**]

handles bulges of extra fat around the waist [C264: love handles]

hands breasts | She's got some big hands.

hang 1. to handle pressure (frequently used in the negative, especially as "can't hang"); to relax, keep cool; to accept or tolerate a situation. 2. to be in a

< > marks words or usages that may be offensive to some or all speakers and that therefore should be used only with discretion; C = Chapman's *New Dictionary of American Slang;* U = previously collected UCLA slang. See the Introduction for more discussion. The Pronunciation Guide provides an explanation of the symbols used in phonetic transcriptions.

place, loiter around | This is so stressful. I can't
hang. | There's nothing to do—let's go hang at the
mall. | —We decided to stay home and watch T.V.
instead of going to a movie. Is that O.K. with you?
—Yeah, I can hang. [C192: (2); hang in 'to endure in
some difficult action or position, persist tena-
ciously'; U83, 87: can't hang. See also **handle**.]

➤   **hang** 1. person who spends a lot of time at
(noun). 2. place where there are a lot of (noun)s
| party hang | Phi Psi hang = person who
spends a lot of time at Phi Psi/place where there
are a lot of Phi Psis

hang a B.A. see **B.A.**

Hang a bootie! 1. Good luck! 2. Wait!
Hold on! | —Come on, Karyn—we're going
to be late. —Hang a bootie! I have to
brush my hair. [See also **be hanging big**
bootie out.]

HANG A BOOTIE!

hang out to relax, take it easy, *kick back,*
veg

hang with 1. to keep company with, stay with.
2. to handle (a situation) | When Sally's date didn't
show up to the party, other couples hung with her
to keep her from feeling lonely. | She turned me
down? Oh, well, I can hang with that.

hanging big bootie out see **be hanging big**
bootie out

hank slut | Every guy in that frat loves her because she's a hank. [C193: 'illicit activity, esp sexual']

HANK

happa 1. person who is half Asian. 2. half-Asian (pronounced [hápə]— rhymes with "cop a") | Joseph's not a pure Filipino —you don't know his dad is German? He's a happa. | She has a happa boyfriend. [<Japanese *hampa* 'half']

happening 1. with it, *hip, cool.* 2. lively, fun (of a party) | That dress is definitely happening; you look great.

happens see **Don't you hate it when that happens? Shit happens!**

happy camper person who is happy or doing O.K.

hard see **Fuck me hard!**

HAPPY CAMPER

harsh very bad, mean | I have a final on my birthday—that's harsh.
➤ **harsh on** to be hard on, be mean to | The professor really harshed on me when I was late for class.

Hasta! See you later! (pronounced [ástə]—rhymes with "pasta") [<Spanish *hasta* 'until']
➤ **Hasta la pasta!** See you later!

< > marks words or usages that may be offensive to some or all speakers and that therefore should be used only with discretion; C = Chapman's *New Dictionary of American Slang;* U = previously collected UCLA slang. See the Introduction for more discussion. The Pronunciation Guide provides an explanation of the symbols used in phonetic transcriptions.

hat see **party hat**

hate see **Don't you hate it when that happens?**

hating life / hating it see **be hating life / be hating it**

haul ass to hurry, to go quickly | Haul ass, dude, I'm already ten minutes late. [C196]

HAUL ASS

have a buzz to have a slightly dizzy feeling as the result of using alcohol, marijuana, or any other drug [C57: buzz 'a feeling or surge of pleasure, esp a pleasant sense of intoxication']

have a C.B. / get a C.B. to be excited | I totally had a C.B. when Josh came into the room. | I got a C.B. when I got my midterm back with an A on it. [<clitoris boner]

have a clue to have an idea, have some information (often used in the negative, as "don't/doesn't have a clue" or sometimes as "have no clue") [C197 chiefly British fr 1940s armed forces: 'to know'. See also **clueless, get a clue, have negative clues.**]

HAVE A CLUE

have a doctor's appointment see **go to the doctor**

have a good personality to be ugly | —How was

your date last night?—He had a good personality.

have a melvin / have melvins / have a murphy
to have one's underwear hiked up [See also **give
(someone) a melvin.**]

have a piece of see **get a piece of**

have cavities to think something is
really nice or sweet | He sent you two
dozen long-stemmed roses? Oh my God—
I have cavities! [See also **give (someone)
cavities.**]

HAVE CAVITIES

have cobwebs not to have had sex for a long time

have cuts to get in front of someone in a line (by
permission of the person one gets in front of) | We
let the cute guys have cuts in the line for the com-
puter. [C92: cut in 'intrude into a conversation'. See
also **give (someone) cuts, take cuts.**]

have missile lock to concentrate on
or make a target of someone (because
of either annoyance or affection) |
Susan picked fights with the team last
year. When she returned this year,
the team said that they had missile
lock. [<the movie *Top Gun*]

HAVE MISSILE LOCK

have negative clues to be completely confused or
completely lacking in common sense | My room-
mate gave me the telephone bill the day after it was

< > marks words or usages that may be offensive to some or all speakers and that therefore
should be used only with discretion; C = Chapman's *New Dictionary of American Slang*; U =
previously collected UCLA slang. See the Introduction for more discussion. The Pronunciation
Guide provides an explanation of the symbols used in phonetic transcriptions.

due. She definitely has negative clues. [See also **clueless, have a clue.**]

have no life to waste time with unimportant things, to have poor priorities, to have a poor social life | He's thirty and still a junior supervisor at McDonald's—he has no life. [See also **Get a life!**]

<**have one's cherry**> to be a virgin (of a woman) [See also **cherry.**]

have __ -orexia to (verb) excessively | That girl has talkorexia. She never shuts up. [<anorexia]

have shotgun see **ride shotgun**

have some see **get some**

Have some __ ! Notice the large number or amount of (noun)! | Have some slang words!

have some V.P.L.s see **have V.P.L.s**

have (someone's) ass to punish, reprimand (someone) | My boss had my ass because I was late three days in a row. [C198]

have the munchies to be uncontrollably hungry, to have an insatiable appetite | My roommates and I rampaged the kitchen when we all got the munchies at the same time. [C200 narcotics & counterculture: 'to be hungry, esp for sweets and starches after using marijuana']

HAVE THE MUNCHIES

have the shits / have the pasties to have diarrhea [C384: the shits 'diarrhea']

have V.B.C. to have the outline of one's buttocks show through very tight clothing | The guy walking in front of us had V.B.C. [<visible butt crack]

have V.P.L.s /have some V.P.L.s to have the outline of one's underpants show through one's clothes (of a female) | The girl standing on the corner had some serious V.P.L.s [<visible panty line]

HAVE V.P.L.s

haze to criticize, insult, *bag on;* to bother | My friend totally hazed me for being late. [U90: 'bother']

head see **airhead, bonehead, bowhead, Brillohead, butthead, deadhead, doughhead, fuckhead, metal head, poohead, pubehead, puderhead, swellhead, talk head**

HAZE

heartbeat see **in a heartbeat**

hearty see **party hearty**

heated drunk, intoxicated | I don't believe that he's in a fraternity if he's heated from three beers.

Heather superficial girl, girl who's a trendy dresser [<the movie *Heathers*]

<> marks words or usages that may be offensive to some or all speakers and that therefore should be used only with discretion; C = Chapman's *New Dictionary of American Slang;* U = previously collected UCLA slang. See the Introduction for more discussion. The Pronunciation Guide provides an explanation of the symbols used in phonetic transcriptions.

heavy deep, profound | I can only talk to Susie for so long; she's too heavy for me. [C202; U83]

➤ **heavily** deeply, seriously

hecka very | You're still studying at this hour? It's hecka late. [<heck of a. See also **hella.**]

<**heifer**> fat girl | Did you see that heifer? She almost plowed into my car and wrecked it! [C203 early 1800s: 'young woman, esp an attractive one']

HEIFER

heinous awful, ugly, unattractive | The girl was wearing the most heinous orange and pink polka-dotted shirt.

hell see **demon from hell, from hell, What the hell?!**

hell master person who is bossy or overly authoritative | The president of the fraternity was a total hell master. He had too many rules and regulations.

HELL MASTER

hella really | You should see that new movie; it's hella cool. [C204: hell of a 'very remarkable'. See also **hecka.**]

hellish rough, difficult, bad | I just had a hellish physics midterm! I know I failed.

Hello! I can't believe this! What's going on here? Ugh! | You put the cat in the fridge? Hello! | I have two hundred pages to read today. Hello!

<**hellpig**> ugly, overweight girl

Hell's bells! / Hell's fire! Damn! Awful! Shit! |
Hell's bells! That was a hard test! [C204 early 1900s:
hell's bells]
➤ **Hell's Bells** someplace really far away | He
lives in Hell's Bells.

hemorrhoid person who is painful to be with; an-
tagonizing person [U84. See also **give (someone)
hemorrhoids.**]

here see **be out of here, Get out of here! What
is the deal?**

Hershey squirt stain on one's underpants due to
a liquid-emitting fart; liquid-emitting fart that
leaves a stain on one's underpants | There were
Hershey squirts all over my brother's underwear. |
My best friend's cat is named Hershey Squirts because it farts so much. They call "Hershey Squirts!"
and I'm all, "Yueechhh!"

hesher person who likes heavy metal music

Hi, Bob! drinking game played while watching
"The Bob Newhart Show"

hick 1. naive person, person who's not
street smart. 2. person who looks out-of-
date or like a farmer or cowboy. 3. person
from a remote (probably rural) suburb, or
somewhere even farther away [C205 late

HICK

< > marks words or usages that may be offensive to some or all speakers and that therefore
should be used only with discretion; C = Chapman's *New Dictionary of American Slang*; U =
previously collected UCLA slang. See the Introduction for more discussion. The Pronunciation
Guide provides an explanation of the symbols used in phonetic transcriptions.

1600s British: 'rural person; a simple, countrified man or woman']

hid ugly, gross [<u>hid</u>eous]

hiddy drunk, intoxicated | Dude, I'm so hiddy I can't even see. [<<u>hid</u>eous]

hide the salami see **play hide the salami**

hip stylish, fashionable, with it, *cool* | Wow, that's a really hip jacket. [C208 beat & cool talk fr black]

hist / histed over, done with, finished [<<u>hist</u>ory; U84: history]
▸ **Hist!** Goodbye!

history see **be history**

hit 1. to take a puff from (a marijuana cigarette or pipe). 2. puff of marijuana | Hit this! | Dude, you look too straight. Do you want a hit? [C209: 'a puff of a marijuana cigarette']
▸ **take a hit** to take a puff of marijuana | Stephanie doesn't party much so it really surprised me when she took a hit off Andrew's joint.

hit on to make a pass at | Then this old man started to hit on me with lines like, "If I was a registered freshman, would I have a chance to get a date with you?" [C209]

ho 1. slutty woman, whore, promiscuous woman. <2. woman.> 3. promiscuous man | By her skimpy clothes we could tell she was a total ho. [<w<u>ho</u>re;

C210: 'prostitute or other disreputable woman']

Hobbes! No bullshit! Swear to God! (pronounced [habz], to rhyme with "jobs") | —You met Paulina last night? Hobbes? —Hobbes! I really did.

hobby horse see **ride the hobby horse**

hockey see **play tonsil hockey**

hoitch female with a displeasing personality (pronounced [hóyč], like "hoy" [rhyming with "boy"], followed by a "ch" sound) | That girl is such a hoitch, she went and told Keith that we were bad-mouthing her. Now he's pissed off and the worst thing is that it's not even true. [<u>ho</u> + <u>bitch</u>]

hold down to wait (*holds down, *held down, *holding down) | Hold down, I'll be ready in two minutes.

Hold the phone! Hold on! Wait a minute! | Hold the phone, I'll be there in a minute. [C212]

Holmes / Homes (term of address for a male) | What's up, Holmes? | Hey, Holmes! [See also **No shit, Sherlock! homeboy.**]

homeboy 1. very close male friend (affectionate term). 2. (term of address for a close male friend) [C213 black: 'close friend'; U87; homeboy 'very close male friend']

HOMEBOY

< > marks words or usages that may be offensive to some or all speakers and that therefore should be used only with discretion; C = Chapman's *New Dictionary of American Slang;* U = previously collected UCLA slang. See the Introduction for more discussion. The Pronunciation Guide provides an explanation of the symbols used in phonetic transcriptions.

➤ **homegirl** 1. very close female friend (affection-ate term). 2. (term of address for a close female friend)

Homes see **Holmes**

homie 1. close, dependable friend, buddy. 2. (term of address) | Susan set me up with her big brother. She's the homie. [<u><homeboy</u>]

<homo> *lame* person, *loser* [<<u>homo</u>sexual. See also **homosexual.**]

<homosexual> strange, odd [See also **gay, homo, queer.**]

honking huge, large | We have a honk-ing textbook in my management class, but the one for English is small.

HONKING

hoof it to walk (usually a long distance) | I drove downtown and couldn't find a parking place. I should have hoofed it. [C214]

hoop / hoops see **shoot hoop**

hork to take without asking, borrow without permission, steal | I couldn't believe he horked my notes right be-fore the test.

HORK

hormone sexually aggressive per-son, person who acts or speaks suggestively | When Mark's hands began to roam, Julie stopped him and called him a hormone.

hormone fix sexual encounter (anything from a make-out session to sexual intercourse) | —So are you seeing Erik now? —No, I just needed a hormone fix.

horse see **ride the hobby horse**

hose female who sleeps with lots of guys [C217: 'cheat, deceive; penis']

➤ **hoser** 1. person who sleeps around. 2. jerk | Bill has slept with three girls this week. What a hoser! [C217: 'person who cheats and deceives'; U84]

hoss stud; muscular male | Gary is such a hoss. His biceps are bigger than my quadriceps. [<Hoss Cartwright, on "Bonanza"]

hot 1. very good, gorgeous, good-looking. 2. wild, slutty (of a female) | The guy I met was so hot that my mouth was left hanging open. | Shelly is so hot it's ridiculous. [C217: 'lively, vital, vibrant'. See also __'s balls are hot, slip (somone) the hot beef injection.]

hound to have sex with | He hounded her last night and now she's totally in love with him! [See also **brewhound.**]

HOUND

house see **brickhouse**

< > marks words or usages that may be offensive to some or all speakers and that therefore should be used only with discretion; C = Chapman's *New Dictionary of American Slang*; U = previously collected UCLA slang. See the Introduction for more discussion. The Pronunciation Guide provides an explanation of the symbols used in phonetic transcriptions.

house plant person who does nothing but sit around the house

How rudeness! / Rudeness! / Rude! How rude! | When I interrupted Jan while she was talking on the phone, she yelled at me, "How rudeness!"

hubby see **husband**

hug the porcelain god / hug the porcelain goddess to vomit into the toilet | Jay drank too much so now he's hugging the porcelain god.

hung hung over

hungry horny

husband / hubby really serious boyfriend

hype *cool,* good

<**hyperdrive whore**> very sleazy girl [See also **turbobitch, turboslut.**]

I i

iced see **get iced**

illin see **be illin**

in a drought see **be in a drought**

in a heartbeat definitely, without hesitation | —Would you go out with Jane? —Oh, in a heartbeat.

in like Flynn all set up, *right in there* | I got a good grade on the midterm—I'm in like Flynn. [C224: 'accepted']

in (someone's) crack see **be in (someone's) crack**

in (someone's) face see **be in (someone's) face, get in (someone's) face**

in the ditch see **be in the ditch**

in there see **be in there**

industrial *studly*, manly | If you can get a date with Bambi, you'll be so industrial, dude!

inebriated drunk, intoxicated

inhale to eat (something) fast | I inhaled my lunch because I didn't have much time to eat. [C225]

INDUSTRIAL

injection see **slip (someone) the hot beef injection**

intense 1. really good, excellent. 2. hard, difficult ➤ Intense! Wow!

into see **be into**

invasion sudden influx of (noun)'s (often used

< > marks words or usages that may be offensive to some or all speakers and that therefore hould be used only with discretion; C = Chapman's *New Dictionary of American Slang*; U = reviously collected UCLA slang. See the Introduction for more discussion. The Pronunciation ;uide provides an explanation of the symbols used in phonetic transcriptions.

alone as a comment on seeing a lot of them) | Blond invasion!

Isn't that special! Big deal! So what! That's not very nice! You think you're so hot! [<"Saturday Night Live"]

Jj

<**jab**> to have sex with (of a male) | He jabbed her.

jack nothing | —What did you do today? —Jack. [C231 esp southern college students: jack shit 'nothing at all']

jack off to masturbate (of a male) [C231]

jacked excited, happy, thrilled | I was really jacked about getting an A on my math test. [C231: jacked up 'stimulated, exhilarated'. See also **jaked**.]

JACKED

jake to cancel an engagement or commitment without notice, flake
➤ **jake on** to stand up, let down, flake on

jaked excited, happy | Bill was jaked because his picture was on the front page of the paper. [See also **jacked**.]

jam 1. to do very well. 2. to hurry; to leave, to get out of here; to go fast, to leave quickly. 3. good song | I jammed

JAM

on my history test. | I'll talk to you later—I've got to jam or I'll be late for class. | That's a jam on the radio. [?C232 esp students fr 1930s black: 'to have a good time'; U84: 'do something well', 83, 84: 'hurry']

➤ **jamming** neat, *cool* | That guy is just the coolest person. I think he is a jamming dude.

jam up to put on the spot | Jane had a talk with Maria about her behavior and really jammed her up. [?C232: 'tight crush of people, cars, etc., preventing normal movement']

Jane see **Mary Jane**

jaw see **blow jaw**

jazzed excited, thrilled, *psyched* | Cynthia was really jazzed that she got an A on her term paper. [C233 teenagers: 'alert and energetic'; U83]

jeek well-dressed, attractive, stylish, *studly, styling* (of a male) (pronounced [jĭk]—rhymes with "week") | Your boyfriend is the raddest dresser; he's so jeek. [<G.Q. See also **G.Q.**]

JEEK

Jell-O see **nail Jell-O to a tree**

"Jeopardy" champion trivia buff

jerk / jerk over to treat disrespectfully, *screw over* | My professor jerked me over when he refused to

< > marks words or usages that may be offensive to some or all speakers and that therefore should be used only with discretion; C = Chapman's *New Dictionary of American Slang*; U = previously collected UCLA slang. See the Introduction for more discussion. The Pronunciation Guide provides an explanation of the symbols used in phonetic transcriptions.

accept my paper two days late. [C234; jerk someone around 'victimize or harass']

➤ **jerk off** to fool around, mess around, not do as one is told

jet to go very fast, to leave quickly | You'd better jet if you want to get there on time. [U84]

jis to ejaculate (pronounced [jĭz]— rhymes with "fizz") [C236: jism 'semen']

JET

job see **Get a job!**

jock 1. to have sex. 2. to have sex with [See also **be on my jock.**]

Jocks see **Rocks for Jocks**

Joe ___ someone male who is characteristically (adjective) | See that guy over there? That's Joe Friendly. Even though I've never met him, he always says "hi" to me when I see him. | Joe Hopeless = someone male who is hopeless for one reason or another | Joe Potential = someone male who could be cute, but he has bad acne, his hair is too long, etc. | [C237: Joe 'man, fellow'. See also **Random Joe.**]

joke see **Location joke!**

jones for to want really badly | She's jonesing for those diamond earrings. [C238: 'any intense interest or absorption']

➤ **joneser** addict (especially to cocaine) | He's become a joneser since he started going out with that girl who deals. [C238: jones 'a drug habit']

judy heavy girl

<**juice**> to have sex with (of a male) | Did you juice her? [See also **precious juice.**]

juke 1. to mess up, *screw over.* 2. to have sex | I got juked by the system. | —Last night I got together with Mark. —Did you juke? —No . . . we just met! [?C239 sports: 'to swerve and reverse evasively; trick a defender or tackler']

jump 1. to beat up. 2. to make a pass at, make a physical move on; to have sex with [C240 late 1800s: 'to attack'; 'to do the sex act with']
➤ **jump on (someone's) bones / jump (someone's) bones** to have sex with, to sexually attack (someone) [U83]

<**just-raped look**> / <**wannabe raped look**> trampy, provocative style of dressing

Kk

K see **Special K pinches**

keg fly person that hangs around the keg at parties

kegger party with kegs of beer | You should go to

: > marks words or usages that may be offensive to some or all speakers and that therefore hould be used only with discretion; C = Chapman's *New Dictionary of American Slang;* U = reviously collected UCLA slang. See the Introduction for more discussion. The Pronunciation uide provides an explanation of the symbols used in phonetic transcriptions.

the kegger at Bill's on Friday night. It should be raging. [C244 teenagers & students: 'beer party']

key 1. very important, essential; good. 2. to scratch the paint off (a vehicle) with a key or another sharp, pointed object | The attendance of cute guys at this party is key. It would definitely be a bummer if only girls showed up. | The car is keyed.

kick ass / kick butt to do very well | I didn't study very much, but I think I kicked ass on my midterm. | Even though Joe thought our midterm was really difficult, I thought I kicked butt. [C245: kick ass 'have power'. See also **butt-kicker.**]

KICK ASS

kick back 1. to relax, calm down. 2. to relax, take it easy | John had nothing to do so he was just kicking back at his apartment. [C245 college students fr black]

kick butt see **kick ass**

kick it to relax, sit down; to hang out [U87]

kick-back unstressed, relaxing | It's a kick-back class. | My Saturday was just so kick-back. I hung out.

kill (someone's) buzz / stomp (someone's) buzz to depress, disappoint (someone) | That's really stomping my buzz. [See also **buzzkill.**]

killer 1. fantastic, *cool, rad.* 2. difficult, bad (of

an experience). 3. very bad experience |
This book is killer. You have to read it. |
That was a killer exam. | That exam was a
killer. [C246: 'person or thing that is re-
markable, wonderful' (adj); U84, 87: 'great,
fantastic']

KILLER

kind / kine see **the kind**

__ **king** male who is very (adjective), (verb)'s a lot,
or has a strong connection with (noun) | He's a
leather jacket king. [See also __ **queen.**]

kinky bizarre-looking [C247: 'dishonest'; middle
1800s: 'eccentric'; 'bizarre'; 'pertaining to sexual de-
viation'; U84]

kiss ass / kiss butt to try to impress, *brownnose;*
to be extremely nice to | My supervisor goes out of
his way to look good in front of the boss. His raise
evaluation is coming up so he's kissing ass to the
boss, hoping to get a high increase in pay. [C247:
kiss ass 'to flatter one's superiors']
➤ **kiss-ass** person who kisses ass, tries to impress people

kiss up to to try to win the favor of (often with
ulterior motives) [See also **kiss ass.**]

knobber blow job [C248: 'male homosexual trans-
vestite prostitute']

< > marks words or usages that may be offensive to some or all speakers and that therefore
should be used only with discretion; C = Chapman's *New Dictionary of American Slang;* U =
previously collected UCLA slang. See the Introduction for more discussion. The Pronunciation
Guide provides an explanation of the symbols used in phonetic transcriptions.

knock boots with to have sex with | He knocked boots with her.

knock the dew off the lily / shake the dew off the lily to urinate (of a male) | Excuse me a minute. I'm going to knock the dew off the lily.

Kodak moment appropriate time for taking pictures | It was a total Kodak moment when the twins fed Jell-O to the dog. [See also **photo opportunity**.]

KODAK MOMENT

kook annoying or mistaken person | He keeps trying to tell me the Chargers are the best team in the NFL. What a kook! | [C251 1950s teenagers: 'eccentric person']

koshe / kosher O.K., neat, *cool* (pronounced [kóš] —rhymes with "gauche") | "How do you like my hairdo?" asked Pepper. "It's koshe," replied Patrick. [<kosher]

Ll

lame stupid, socially inept, clumsy, awkward, unsuccessful, half-hearted | Cindy normally tells such great jokes but that last one was really lame. | That class was so lame—all we did was copy notes off the board and memorize them. [C253: 'inept'; U83, 84]

last call look desperate look guys get when a bar announces last call for alcohol and they haven't found a girl to go home with yet | My friends like to leave the club before one-thirty to avoid the guys with the last call look in their eyes.

LAST CALL
LOOK

Later! / Lates! / Late! goodbye, see you later | —I have to get going, Paul. —O.K., later. | Lates, Dave, I'll see you in class tomorrow. [C254 esp teenagers fr black: later; U84: later]

➤ **Later!** Shut up! You're weird! Enough of that!

laying pipe see **be laying pipe**

league see **bush-league, major-league**

leech person who will not leave some-one alone; *mooch;* person who lives off or is supported by another person without giving anything in return | Kathy is such a leech. I can't shake her for five min-utes. [C256: 'human parasite']

LEECH

leg see **third leg**

let one go to pass gas, fart (does not have to be audible) | Mary was so em-barrassed—by accident she let one go in the movie theater and everyone around her moved to different seats.

➤ **let one rip / rip one /rip** to pass

LET ONE GO

< > marks words or usages that may be offensive to some or all speakers and that therefore should be used only with discretion; C = Chapman's *New Dictionary of American Slang;* U = previously collected UCLA slang. See the Introduction for more discussion. The Pronunciation Guide provides an explanation of the symbols used in phonetic transcriptions.

gas, fart (audibly) | During my psychology mid-term, the guy behind me let one rip. It was so disgusting!

Let's vamos! Let's go! [<Spanish *vamos* 'let's go']

LET'S VAMOS!

lick see **buttlick**

<Lick me!> Shut up! You make me sick! Get out of here! Kiss my ass! *Fuck you!*

Lick my love pump! Shut up! You make me sick! Get out of here! Kiss my ass! *Fuck you!*

life see **be hating life, be loving life, Get a life! have no life**

lifejacket condom

lightweight person with a low tolerance for alcohol | Tony drank one beer and was totally blitzed—what a lightweight.

like 1. (word used to emphasize or call attention to a following phrase). 2. just. 3. um. 4. about, more or less | Like where are you going? | It was like totally gross. | My tie only cost like ten dollars. [C259 esp 1960s counterculture & bop talk: 'really; you know; sort of'. See also **be like, in like Flynn.**]

like a mojo a lot | He was scoring like a mojo. [C280 black: mojo 'charm or amulet worn against evil; hence, power, luck, effectiveness']

like five miles of bad road like something really awful

LIKE FIVE MILES OF BAD ROAD

lily see **knock the dew off the lily**

lit drunk, intoxicated; high on cocaine | He loves to dance when he's lit. | Every time Vanna walks out on "Wheel of Fortune" she looks like she's lit. [C261. See also **Shit Lit.**]

live *cool* | The decor in that apartment is live, I love it. (pronounced [láyv], like "live," as in "alive") [C261 esp teenagers: 'lively, exciting']

load up to get high or drunk | John always loads up before he goes to fraternity parties.

➤ **loaded** high, stoned, drunk, intoxicated | Jerry got so loaded at the party last night that we were afraid to let him drive home. [C261]

Location joke! You had to be there!

LOCATION JOKE!

lock see **have missile lock**

look see **last call look**

lookie-lou nosy person (pronounced [lʊ́ki lu]—"lookie" rhymes with "cookie," plus "lou") [U83: 'boy- or girl-watcher']

loon weird person | Karen doesn't like ice cream. What a loon! [C87: crazy as a loon 'insane'; 263 looney, loon: 'crazy' (noun)]

< > marks words or usages that may be offensive to some or all speakers and that therefore should be used only with discretion; C = Chapman's *New Dictionary of American Slang*; U = previously collected UCLA slang. See the Introduction for more discussion. The Pronunciation Guide provides an explanation of the symbols used in phonetic transcriptions.

loose very drunk, almost passed out [See also **get loose.**]

lose it 1. to be surprised, to lose one's composure; to go out of control, be unable to cope. 2. to vomit | I was losing it last week with three midterms. [C265: lose one's cool 'become angry or flustered, lose composure']

LOSE IT

loser 1. failure, especially a social failure. 2. bad, awful | That guy in my biophysics class is such an incredible loser! | I can't believe you get all these loser classes. [C264: 'person or thing that fails'. See also **wicked loser.**]

lou / louis ugly guy | He's such a lou. [See also **lookie-lou.**]

love see **make love to the porcelain goddess**

love pump see **Lick my love pump!**

lovebite hickey | Dan couldn't cover the lovebite on his neck with a turtleneck.

<lovesteak> penis | *Playgirl* always has men with big lovesteaks as their centerfolds. [See also **tubesteak of love.**]

LOVEBITE

loving life / loving it see **be loving life**

lowlife pledge or neophyte member of a fraternity | The lowlifes have to clean the floors, reconstruct the roof, and repaint the house before they become actives.

lump 1. useless, lazy person. 2. to be useless and lazy | He's a total lump; he never moves. | We just lumped all afternoon. It was so relaxing! [C266: 'dull, stupid person']

lush 1. person who drinks a lot. 2. drunk, intoxicated. 3. sexually attractive | Mary is such a lush. She can't go to a party without getting drunk. [C267 late 1800s: 'drunkard'; lushed 'drunk']

M m

mac / mac out to eat something, have some food (usually, a lot) | Let's go mac. | He really macked out last night. [<McDonald's. See also **make mac with.**]

➤ **mac on** to eat | We'll mac on hamburgers and fries tonight.

maggot extremely lazy person, who may not even get out of bed all day [See also **sloth.**]

magnet see **babe magnet**

Magoo person driving a car slowly (especially, an

< > marks words or usages that may be offensive to some or all speakers and that therefore should be used only with discretion; C = Chapman's *New Dictionary of American Slang*; U = previously collected UCLA slang. See the Introduction for more discussion. The Pronunciation Guide provides an explanation of the symbols used in phonetic transcriptions.

old man) | There's a Magoo in front of us. [<the cartoon character Mr. Magoo]

main vein see **drain the dragon**

major extreme, complete and total, important, big | My roommate's boyfriend is a major nerd, complete with polyester pants, a plastic pocket protector, and slicked-back hair. | I have the major headache. [See also **flake major**.]

MAJOR

➤ **major time** to an intense degree, a lot | I had to study major time. | There's potato chips major time here.

➤ **majorly** extremely, really, a lot | My mechanical engineering class is majorly hard—I'll be lucky to get a C. | I am majorly stressed about the exam on Tuesday.

➤ **major-league** 1. total, real, *big time.* 2. many, a lot of | That guy has failed five classes, a major-league loser. | There's major-league potato chips here. [See also **bush-league**.]

make a fashion arrest to accuse someone of dressing unfashionably, criticize someone's dress (usually not to his or her face) | When I saw Belinda in her pink spandex miniskirt, I decided to make a fashion arrest. [See also **arrest**.]

MAKE A
FASHION ARREST

make a pit stop to go into a bathroom (for any

purpose) [C271: 'urinate']

➤ **make a piss stop** to go into a bathroom to urinate

make love to the porcelain goddess to vomit into the toilet | I have the feeling that I'm going to be making love to the porcelain goddess for a while tonight.

make mac with to flirt with, to *come on to* | I am going to go to the party and try to make mac with Lisa. She is really cute.

make (someone) scream to have sex with (someone)

mama see **freak mama**

MAKE MAC WITH

man see **budman, Dude man! missionary man, Three Man, working man's smile, yeah-man**

mangled unkempt, disheveled, *thrashed* | Susan looked mangled after her date with Mark.

marks see **Do you see skid marks on my forehead?**

married see **be married**

Mary Jane marijuana [English form of María Juana; C274. See also **M.J.**]

mash to kiss, neck, make out | My blind date and

< > marks words or usages that may be offensive to some or all speakers and that therefore should be used only with discretion; C = Chapman's *New Dictionary of American Slang*; U = previously collected UCLA slang. See the Introduction for more discussion. The Pronunciation Guide provides an explanation of the symbols used in phonetic transcriptions.

I felt just a little uncomfortable when you guys started mashing in the back seat last night. [C274 middle 1800s: 'to make a sexual advance to']

MASH

➤ **mash with** to make out with, neck with, kiss

maul to make out fervently | The ho at the party was mauling with every guy there.

mazeh gorgeous guy (pronounced [mazé]—rhymes with "pause A") | Mel Gibson is a total mazeh. [<Hebrew *ma ze* 'what is this?']
➤ **mazehette** gorgeous girl (pronounced [mazɛ́t] —rhymes with "pause-ette")

McFly person with no intelligence, *airhead* | "You McFly," Bob said when Sue said a dumb thing. [<George McFly, a character in *Back to the Future*]
➤ **McFly!** Wake up!

McPaper poor, hurriedly written paper done without much research or forethought [<McDonald's]

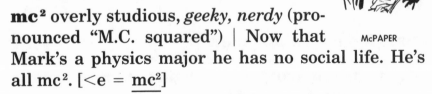

McPAPER

mc² overly studious, *geeky, nerdy* (pronounced "M.C. squared") | Now that Mark's a physics major he has no social life. He's all mc². [<e = mc^2]

me see **Bite me! C.F.M., Eat me! Fuck me! Fuck me hard! fuck-me boots, fuck-me eyes, Lick me! Stoke me!**

___ **me** give me (a/an/some) (noun) (for some speakers, this can be used with other pronouns, but it's most common with "me") | "Pen me," Julie said to the bank teller when she cashed her check.

mega 1. extreme, large. 2. very. 3. a lot of | I have the mega headache. | I'm mega tired. | I have mega homework. [C275 esp students & teenagers: 'much' (adv)]

___ **-meister** person who is heavily associated in some way with (noun) / (verb)-ing (sometimes the word in the blank may be shortened) | Dave's habit of saying, "Dude, you're stewed!" led our floor to call him stewmeister. | kegmeister | suspendermeister [See also **monster.**]

mellow calm; quiet | Tommy, you're so mellow tonight—is something bothering you? [C276]
➤ **mellow out** to relax, to *veg* | Let's just go mellow out at your apartment tonight. I'm too tired to go out. [C276; U84: 'calm down']

melvin / melvins see **give (someone) a melvin, have a melvin**

mental giant / mental midget unintelligent person | I locked my keys in my car again. What a mental giant!

mess up 1. to make a mistake, do badly. 2. to beat up | I messed up on my math final and it might cost me my grade. [C276: mess up 'to disarrange; muddle'; 'to injure, damage']

➤ **messed up** drunk, intoxicated; high on drugs; mean, *screwed* | He was so messed up that he couldn't walk straight.

metal head person who likes heavy metal music

Mexicali / Mexico drinking game played with dice

MEXICALI

M.F. extremely rotten, low person | That lousy M.F. stole my car stereo. [<mother-erfucker]

mick 1. easy class. 2. easy, simple | I heard that Astro 3 is a mick. Everyone gets As. | Russian 27A is a mick course. [<Mickey Mouse; C277 college students: Mickey Mouse 'simple, elementary, easy'; U87]

microblast to microwave

midget see **mental giant**

Midol see **Take a Midol!**

miffed very angry or upset | Sarah was miffed that she waited two hours in line to buy just one book. [C278 early 1800s: 'angered, upset']

MIFFED

mike see **talk to the mike**

miles see **like five miles of bad road**

Miller time time to have a drink | Sometimes I say it's Miller time when all I want is a Dr. Pepper. [<the Miller beer commercial]

<**mindfuck**> 1. to deceive, tease; to play with (someone's) mind. 2. person who *mindfucks* [C278: 'manipulate someone to think and act as one wishes']
➤ <**mindfucked**> drunk, intoxicated

Miss ___ / Mrs. ___ female who characteristically (verb)'s, female associated with (noun) (either term can be used, without regard to the person's marital status) | Miss Mooch always grabs ten cookies. [See also **Mr. ___ , Ms. ___ .**]

missile lock see **have missile lock**

mission see **be on a mission**

missionary man boring sexual part-ner [<the missionary position]

M.J. marijuana [<marijuana; C280. See also **Mary Jane.**]

MISSIONARY MAN

mockery farce, something open to rid-icule | Jon started jumping that ugly girl the other night. What a mockery! [See also **buffoonery.**]

moded see **molded**

mojo see **like a mojo**

mold to humiliate, to catch in a contradiction or mistake

➤ **molded / moded** humiliated (usually publicly), having things not work out for one | Since I'd bragged about having the highest grade in the class, I was moded when I got a D on the final. [U84: get moded 'get caught, get in trouble and not be able to get out of it']

➤ **moldy** see **come out moldy, feel moldy**

Molester see **Chester Molester**

moment see **Kodak moment**

Monday night attire dressy clothes, such as might be worn to church or a nice restaurant (sorority and fraternity term) | "What should I wear to my interview?" Suzy asked. "Wear Monday night attire," said her friend.

MONDAY
NIGHT
ATTIRE

mondo / mongo 1. very. 2. big | Your dad is mondo cool! | I've got a mongo bruise on my leg from field hockey. [? C281: mongo 'something valuable found in the garbage']

monkey other woman or man in a boyfriend's or girlfriend's life | I've heard Mitch is cheating on me. When I find his monkey, I'm going to do her up! [?C281: monkey business 'frivolous pranks']

monkey bite hickey

MONKEY

__-**monster** person who is associated with (noun)'s or has a tendency to (verb) | miniskirtmonster | munchiemonster | studymonster | partymonster [U87. See also __-**meister, P.M.S. monster.**]

monthly bill menstrual period | I got my monthly bill yesterday.

MONTHLY BILL

mooch 1. person who always uses other people's things, constant borrower. 2. to take, borrow things (as a general rule) | You're such a mooch! Get your own lunch! [C282 middle 1500s British: 'to beg, to borrow' (n)]
➤ **mooch off** to take, borrow from

M.O.S. member of the opposite sex

mosquito bites small breasts

motor to leave [U83: 'go by car or motorized vehicle']

mount to have sex with | She mounted him.

mouthbreather very stupid person | Will all of the mouthbreathers leave so that we can get some work done? [C284]

MOUNT

Mouth-O! This tastes great! [<orgasm]

move see **bust a move**

mow to eat until one bursts, gorge oneself | Raquel

<> marks words or usages that may be offensive to some or all speakers and that therefore should be used only with discretion; C = Chapman's *New Dictionary of American Slang;* U = previously collected UCLA slang. See the Introduction for more discussion. The Pronunciation Guide provides an explanation of the symbols used in phonetic transcriptions.

hadn't eaten all day, so when Bob took her to dinner, she mowed. [U84]

Mr. __ male who characteristically (verb)'s, male associated with (noun) [See also **Miss** __.]

➤ **Mr. Groin** promiscuous male, male with a reputation for being lascivious | Charlie has different girls spend the night on a regular basis. I swear, he's a Mr. Groin.

Mr. Smith drinking game with complicated rules in which one player is a dictator named Mr. Smith who directs the others' behavior

MR. SMITH

Mrs. __ see **Miss** __

Ms. __ female who characteristically (verb)'s, female associated with (noun) (has a '70s ring) [See also **Miss** __, **Mr.** __.]

muffy person who looks like a sorority girl (incredibly superficial, usually with bleached blond hair, lots of makeup, and a hair bow)

mufugly very ugly, *fugly* (pronounced [məfʌgli], like "muff" plus "fugly") [<mother-fucking ugly. See also **fugly.**]

MULTIPLE SADNESS!

Multiple sadness! Oh no! That's too bad! | You overslept and missed your final this morning? Dude, multiple sadness!

munch 1. to crash, mess up, *mangle*. 2. to do

poorly on | When Johnny got in that accident, he munched his motorcycle and his face.

muncher see **carpet muncher**

munchies see **have the munchies**

mung filth or dirt of any kind (under the couch, spilled on the table, etc.) [C285 esp teenagers]

➤ **mung rag** towel for cleaning *mung*

murder very difficult | That exam was so murder! I'll be stoked if I even passed. | That was a murder exam. [C285: 'a very difficult person or thing']

murphy see **have a melvin**

musical __ see **play musical __**

mutant outcast | Marvin is a mutant—he is constantly picking his nose in public. [See also **fashion criminal**.]

MUTANT

my see **be on my jock, be on my tit, Get out of my face! Lick my love pump!**

Nn

N No (condescending negative response) | —Won't you please let us come with you? —N.

nads testicles [<go<u>nads</u>]

< > marks words or usages that may be offensive to some or all speakers and that therefore should be used only with discretion; C = Chapman's *New Dictionary of American Slang*; U = previously collected UCLA slang. See the Introduction for more discussion. The Pronunciation Guide provides an explanation of the symbols used in phonetic transcriptions.

nail <1. to have sex with.> 2. to catch (someone) in the wrong. 3. to do well on, *ace* | He nailed her. | I have to nail my math midterm. I can't afford to bomb this one too. [(1, 2) C289; (3) C289 nail down 'make something securely final'; 'know thoroughly']

nail Jell-O to a tree to do the impossible

nappy 1. tired. 2. dirty, messy, neglected (especially, of hair) | I was so nappy after work that I fell asleep on my bed at six P.M. and I didn't wake up until midnight. | —Eeeewhh, Kelly's panties are nappy. —No doubt! She's been wearing them for a week.

Nasal no
➤ **Nasal on that!** Forget that!

nasty 1. gorgeous, sexually attractive. 2. gross | "Did you see Karen at the party last night?" Doug asked.

NASAL

"She looked nasty!" [C290 black: 'good, stylish, admirable'. See also **do the deed.**]

nectar 1. outstanding, *awesome, sweet.* 2. alcoholic beverage | Paul scored an incredible goal in the soccer game. It was nectar. | It was a nectar game. | Ahh, nectar.

negative see **have negative clues**

nerd person who studies a lot or is socially outdated, misfit, *geek, dweeb;* jerk [C290 teenagers fr hot rodders & surfers: 'tedious, contemptible person']

➤ **nerdy** characteristic of a nerd [C290 teenagers]

newt inept or inexperienced person, *wimp* | Adrian can't get girls 'cause he's such a newt.

N.G.B. nice guy one's not interested in [nice guy but]

N.G.B.

nibble at to argue with mildly | —Were you two fighting yesterday? —No, we were just nibbling at each other.

nibbling somewhat cold (of the weather), chilly | You won't need both a sweatshirt and a jacket when you go out tonight—it's only nibbling outside.

nifty neat, great | That's a nifty sweater you're wearing. [C291 middle 1800s]

night attire see **Monday night attire**

nightie bad experience beyond one's control; ugly person | I had three finals today. What a nightie! [<nightmare + ie]

nightmare 1. bad experience beyond one's control. 2. ugly person. 3. ugly | I studied so hard for my midterm, but I did terribly. It was a nightmare. | She was a nightmare date. [U84]

NIGHTMARE

nisty very ugly | Look at her disgusting face! She's nisty!

< > marks words or usages that may be offensive to some or all speakers and that therefore should be used only with discretion; C = Chapman's *New Dictionary of American Slang;* U = previously collected UCLA slang. See the Introduction for more discussion. The Pronunciation Guide provides an explanation of the symbols used in phonetic transcriptions.

nix to remove from consideration, to turn down for or remove (someone) from a position, to fire | That word shouldn't go on our list; nix it! | I worked there for nine years before they nixed me. [C293: 'veto, reject']

No biggie! No problem, no big deal, no sweat, don't worry about it [U83]

NO BIGGIE!

No bitch! I don't have to sit in the middle of the back seat! (exclamation used after someone else has claimed "Shotgun!") [See also **ride bitch.**]

No Cool Northern California [See also **So Cool.**]

No doubt! Definitely! For sure! | Are you stressed about finals? I am, no doubt!

no life see **have no life**

No shit! Really! Of course! Tell me something I don't already know! No way! Are you serious? | —Did you know Sam won ten thousand dollars instantly on the lottery? —No shit!

➤ **No shit, Sherlock!** No kidding! Tell me something I don't already know! | —Did you know that the Rose Bowl is in Pasadena? —No shit, Sherlock! [See also **Holmes.**]

No way! Wow! | —I got an A. —No way! [C296: 'no, absolutely not']

No wire hangers! / No more wire hangers! Don't make me do this! NO WIRE HANGERS!

How terrible! That *sucks*! | I have class Monday night, oh no wire hangers! [<Joan Crawford's remark in *Mommie Dearest*, perhaps influenced by a prochoice slogan]

noise see **Fuck that noise!**

nose see **brownnose**

nosh 1. to snack, have a snack. 2. snack [<Yiddish *nosh* 'to snack on nonnourishing foods'; C295]

➤ **nosh on** to snack on | When I came home from school I noshed on some cookies until dinnertime.

NOSH

Not! No! You've got to be kidding! | —I have been having so much fun at all of the parties. —But you've gotten a lot of homework done? —Not!

not even not at all | —My bio professor canceled our final and is going to give everyone an A. —You're not even serious! I just dropped that class.

➤ **Not even!** No way! You're kidding! | —That chick is way dyno. —Not even! I've seen her in a bikini.

nugget fool, idiot

nuke to microwave; to burn; to blow-dry excessively | My soup got cold. Will you nuke it for me? [C297; 'to destroy'; U87]

NUKE

< > marks words or usages that may be offensive to some or all speakers and that therefore should be used only with discretion; C = Chapman's *New Dictionary of American Slang*; U = previously collected UCLA slang. See the Introduction for more discussion. The Pronunciation Guide provides an explanation of the symbols used in phonetic transcriptions.

➤ **nuke oneself** to go to a tanning salon

➤ **nuker** microwave oven | Put the food in the nuker and I'll take it out for you.

nummy yummy | Oh, these cookies are so nummy, I could eat all of them.

nun unaffectionate girl or woman, prudish girl who doesn't put out at all | No, I'll never go out with her. I hear she's a total nun—get none!

NUN

O o

ob 1. obvious. 2. obviously | That's so ob! | Ob not! [<u><obvious</u>(ly)]

obliterated drunk, intoxicated | The chick at the Everclear party was completely obliterated.

obno obnoxious (pronounced [óbno]—first syllable rhymes with "lobe," second like "no") [<obnoxious]

➤ **obnoc** obnoxious (pronounced [ábnak], like the beginning of "obnoxious") | That music is so obnoc. Please turn it off. [<u><obnoc</u>-sious]

obscure peculiar, odd | You came back to your apartment and your door was wide open? That's so obscure!

Odd or Even drinking game involving guessing whether another player will hold up an odd or even number of fingers

off see **get off**

off one's ass to the most extreme degree, in a big way (used with words for 'drunk' or 'tired') | My roommate was wasted off his ass by the time the party was over, and I had to carry him to bed.

___**-oholic** person who (verb)'s all the time, person who is preoccupied with (noun) | shopoholic | stressoholic | partyoholic | slangoholic

___**-ola** 1. really (adjective), characterized by (noun). 2. *total* (noun/adjective) | studola | grossola | barfola [C303: -ola: 'an emphatic instance or humorous version of what is indicated' (suffix used to form nouns)]

old battle-ax ex-girlfriend | My old battle-ax started dating my best friend.

on fire doing well, on a roll | The basketball team has won eight straight—they're on fire. [See also **fire up.**]

on my jock see **be on my jock**

on my tit see **be on my tit**

on (someone's) ass see **be on (someone's) ass**

on the rag 1. <in a bad mood, acting unfriendly.> 2. having a menstrual period | Joe's been on the rag for the past week; all he does is yell. [(2) C307; (1)

< > marks words or usages that may be offensive to some or all speakers and that therefore should be used only with discretion; C = Chapman's *New Dictionary of American Slang;* U = previously collected UCLA slang. See the Introduction for more discussion. The Pronunciation Guide provides an explanation of the symbols used in phonetic transcriptions.

U83, 84: 'in a bad mood, acting unfriendly']

one bagger ugly person (so ugly you need to put a bag over his or her head) [See also **bagger, two bagger.**]

oochie cute person | Michael J. Fox is a total oochie.

__**-o-rama** / __**-rama** 1. totally (adjective). 2. absolute (noun). 3. event or condition characterized by lots of (noun) or by (verb)-ing [Usually, -o-rama follows words ending in an accented syllable and -rama follows words ending in an unaccented syllable. Normally, adjective+ -o-rama = adjective, noun+ -o-rama = noun; occasionally, though, other relationships are possible, and verb+ -o-rama may produce verbs that cannot be inflected.] | The food they serve at my dorm is gross-o-rama. | That guy over by the punch bowl is a babe-o-rama. | We had a real munch-o-rama. | Let's go munch-o-rama. | I've got blister-rama. [C353: 'spectacular display or instance of what is indicated' (suffix used to form nouns)]

oozing scabs any venereal disease | Tony was so gross, I hope he didn't give me oozing scabs.

opportunity see **photo opportunity**

orange banana flaring of a lighted match when someone passes gas close to it

ORANGE BANANA

___ **-orexia** see **have ___-orexia**

orgasm <to be in a state of euphoria> | The con-
cert was so great I orgasmed.
➤ **orgasmic** extremely pleasing to the senses |
   The mud pie they serve at the Charthouse is
   just orgasmic.

O.T.R. *on the rag,* in a bad mood | Stay away from
her today, she's O.T.R. [<on the rag]

out see **be out of here, be out of there, Check
it out! Get out of my face!**

out of control 1. drunk, intoxicated. 2. over-
reacting, *stressed, wired.* 3. wild | Carol's dress is
out of control.

over see **be all over, be over**

Pp

pack <to have sex (of male homosexuals)> | Ron
and Don packed all night long.
➤ **packer** <homosexual male>

painful bad

paper see **McPaper**

party 1. to drink alcohol (with others), celebrate, go to a party. 2. to take drugs: es-

PAINFUL

< > marks words or usages that may be offensive to some or all speakers and that therefore
should be used only with discretion; C = Chapman's *New Dictionary of American Slang;* U =
previously collected UCLA slang. See the Introduction for more discussion. The Pronunciation
Guide provides an explanation of the symbols used in phonetic transcriptions.

pecially, to smoke marijuana. 3. to take (a drug) in a social situation | Finals are over! Let's party! | Are we going to party dolomite tonight? [C316: 'go to or give parties': 'enjoy oneself drinking, chatting, dancing, etc.'; U83, 87]

party favors narcotics, drugs

party foul 1. to do something inap-propriate or rude at a party or social gathering: especially, to vomit or spill alcohol. 2. inappropriate act at a party or fashion faux pas (often used as an exclamation) | John party fouled big time when he spilled his drink all over the white carpet. | There was no food at the dance. Party foul!

PARTY FAVORS

party hat condom | After three long weeks Biff finally got a girl to go home with him. In the heat of the moment, he realized he didn't have a party hat.

party hearty to have a good time at a party, *rage*

Party on! 1. keep *partying*! 2. Have a good time! 3. Good job! [See also **Rock out!**]

PARTY ON

party sci political science (sci is pronounced [say], like "sigh") [<u>political science</u>]

pasta see **Hasta la pasta!**

pasties see **have the shits**

pasty very pale or white (of skin, especially with big pink splotches)

peeps see **Ps**

penetration sexual intercourse | "Was there penetration?" Christie asked when Janet returned from her date with Mark.

<**penis wrinkle**> male jerk

penny a door to stick pennies in the crack of the outside of a door where the hinges are and thus prevent the door from being opened from the inside
➤ **penny in** to keep (someone) in a room by pennying the door | They pennied him in.

People see **Pretty People U.**

perm see **give (someone) a perm**

perpetrate to act fraudulently or in an illegitimate way [U89]
➤ **perpetrate like** to pretend that | People get fake antennas to perpetrate like they have a car phone.
➤ **perpetrator** fake person, *wannabe*

person see **random person**

personality see **have a good personality**

phone see **Hold the phone! talk to Ralph on the big white phone**

< > marks words or usages that may be offensive to some or all speakers and that therefore should be used only with discretion; C = Chapman's *New Dictionary of American Slang*; U = previously collected UCLA slang. See the Introduction for more discussion. The Pronunciation Guide provides an explanation of the symbols used in phonetic transcriptions.

phony 1. bad; not good. 2. crank or prank phone call | That movie starring Tom Cruise was really phony. | I'm thinking of changing my phone number because I've been getting a lot of phonies recently. [C321 late 1800s: 'not real or genuine, false, fake'; (2) influenced by phone]

photo opportunity appropriate time for taking pictures [See also **Kodak moment.**]

photog person who takes a lot of pic-tures; professional photographer at a party (pronounced [fótag], like "foe" plus "tog") | When Suzy finished her tenth roll of film, Lori said, "You are a total photog. We should hire you for our next sorority party!"

PHOTOG

pickled drunk, intoxicated

picture See **Take a picture!**

piece 1. hairstyle, hairdo. 2. something undesir-able | Dave's got a rad piece. It's fuschia. | Your rusty, dented '77 Nova is a real piece. [(1) ?<hair-piece; (2) U90. See also **piece of shit.**]

piece of see **get a piece of**

piece of chickenshit coward, *wimp*, chickenshit [See also **chickenshit, piece of shit.**]

piece of shit poor, low quality | That's a piece of shit radio. [C322: 'something inferior or worthless']

pieces see **Did you get any pieces?**

pig / pig out to eat a lot, gorge oneself |
We were hungry last night, so we ordered
a pizza and totally pigged out. [C323 teenagers: pig out; U83: pig out. See also
bushpig, hellpig.]

PIG

➤ **pig on / pig out on** to eat a lot of | At
her birthday party, I pigged out on chocolate
ice cream.

pile <1. to have sex.> <2. to have sex with>

pill see **take a chill pill**

pimp to dress very nicely | The party is
semiformal; I can't wait to pimp for it!

➤ **pimping / pimping it** doing well,
looking good

pinches see **Special K pinches**

PIMP

pine see **ride the pine**

pinned high on cocaine | The actor was so pinned,
he rubbed his nose twenty-two times in a minute.
[C325 narcotics: 'contracted' (of the pupils)]

pinner 1. thin (of a person or a part of the body).
2. thin person | Rick has pinner legs. | Look at Jenn
—she is such a pinner.

pirate see **butt pirate**

< > marks words or usages that may be offensive to some or all speakers and that therefore
should be used only with discretion; C = Chapman's *New Dictionary of American Slang;* U =
previously collected UCLA slang. See the Introduction for more discussion. The Pronunciation
Guide provides an explanation of the symbols used in phonetic transcriptions.

pirate's dream flat-chested woman (with a sunken chest) | Judy is such a pirate's dream, she's twenty-four and still wears a training bra.

piss off 1. to beat it, go away. 2. to upset, anger (?pissed off ("rare"), *pissing off) | This barney asked my roommate out every night until she finally told him to piss off. | My roommates piss me off when they don't do their dishes. [C327: piss someone off 'to make angry, arouse indignation']
➤ **Piss off!** Go away! Shut up!

piss ugly very ugly

pissed / pissed off angry, upset | I'm so pissed. My birthday is the day before finals. [U83; pissed 'angry'; 83, 87: pissed off 'angry']
➤ **pissed / pissed up** drunk, intoxicated

PISSED

pizza face person with severe acne | I was surprised when I met Scott; I'd heard he was good-looking, but he was actually a total pizza face.

plant see **house plant**

plastered drunk, intoxicated | That party was a blast—I was so plastered. [C328; U84]

plastic phony, superficial [C328 esp 1960s counterculture]

<play hide the salami> to have sex | On our date Friday night, Craig suggested that we play hide the salami.

PLASTIC

[C329: play hide the weenie]

play hoops see **shoot hoop**

play musical __ to switch around among different (noun)'s a lot or at random | play musical beds = to choose sex partners at random and very often; to sleep around | play musical classes = to try out many classes, to switch around between classes | My roommate played musical beds all quarter; we never saw the same guy twice. [C286: musical beds 'sexual promiscuity']

PLAY MUSICAL ___

play the skin flute to perform oral sex on a male; to masturbate (of a male)

play tonsil hockey to deep, deep kiss | He's always trying to play tonsil hockey, so I feel like I'm getting suffocated.

player promiscuous person [C329]

plowed drunk, intoxicated

plug <to have sex with (of a male)>

PLOWED

P.M.S. premidterm stress [premidterm stress, based on P.M.S., premenstrual syndrome]

P.M.S. monster menstruating woman [<P.M.S. / premenstrual syndrome]

< > marks words or usages that may be offensive to some or all speakers and that therefore should be used only with discretion; C = Chapman's *New Dictionary of American Slang;* U = previously collected UCLA slang. See the Introduction for more discussion. The Pronunciation Guide provides an explanation of the symbols used in phonetic transcriptions.

poke <to have sex with (of a male)> [C332; U84]

police see **fashion police**

polluted drunk, intoxicated

pond scum see **shower scum**

poohead person who's getting on one's nerves, nuisance | Stephanie, will you quit playing the drums? You're being a poohead.

POLLUTED

pooper (female's) rear end, buttocks | She's cute but she has a big pooper.

pop 1. to punch, smack. 2. to impregnate. 3. to give (someone) his or her first experience with something (smoking, drugs, sex, etc.), *devirginize* [C334: 'do the sex act with'. See also **popped**.]

pop off to brag, boast; to make critical remarks, say negative things | He was popping off too much about his basketball abilities, so I played him a game and slammed him. | I don't know why my dad is always popping off about my clothes. [C335: 'to talk loudly and perhaps prematurely']

popped in a bad situation | The policeman behind us just turned on his lights. Now we're going to get popped. [C324 students: pop 'catch']

porcelain see **bow to the porcelain god, drive the bus, hug the porcelain god, make love to the porcelain goddess,**

POPPED

pray to the porcelain god, worship the porcelain god

pork / pork out to eat a lot | My friends and I always pork out when we go to Sizzler and get the all-you-can-eat salad bar. | We fully porked after the game. [C335: pork out]

➤ **pork on / pork out on** to eat a lot of | Debbie and I porked out on the brownies that her mom made for us.

porker fat person; person who eats a lot

poser / poseur really fake person, *wannabe*

posse group of friends, best friend

POSSE

pound / power to drink (beer) rapidly | Jerry pounded an entire six-pack of beer before the party even started. | The movie starts in ten minutes. Come on, power that six-pack.

powder cocaine

power see **pound**

power on / power through to do well on | You're going to power on that exam. [C337 baseball: power 'hit the ball very hard']

powerstudy to study hard

P.P.D. attractive person of the opposite sex [<pos-

< > marks words or usages that may be offensive to some or all speakers and that therefore should be used only with discretion; C = Chapman's *New Dictionary of American Slang;* U = previously collected UCLA slang. See the Introduction for more discussion. The Pronunciation Guide provides an explanation of the symbols used in phonetic transcriptions.

sible/potential prom date. See also **prom date.**]

pray to the porcelain god / pray to the porcelain goddess to vomit into the toilet | You should have seen Keith Saturday! He was praying to the porcelain goddess all night!

precious juice alcoholic beverage | Don't spill the precious juice, because there's hardly any left.

preg pregnant [<pregnant; C337; preggy, prego; U90: preggo]

pretty ridiculous, *bogus* | We're stuck out here in the middle of nowhere with no gas. Well, that's pretty.

Pretty People U. a university whose students are predominantly attractive and well-dressed | M.I.T. is certainly not Pretty People U.

prick <jerk; mean, offensive, inconsiderate, rude, or unfair person (usually, a male)> | Carrie's boyfriend cheated on her. What a prick.

<**pricktease**> / **P.T.** woman who flirts with a man, turns him on, and later shows no interest in him | That girl has a reputation for being a P.T. Guys should know to stay away from her. [C76: prickteaser 'woman ... who arouses a man sexually by granting certain favors, then denies him the sex act'. See also **dicktease.**]

primo 1. great, awesome. 2. marijuana joint laced

with cocaine | I had a primo time at the party. I've never had so much fun. [U90 (1)]

prom date unattractive person of the opposite sex [See also **P.P.D.**]

PROM DATE

Ps / peeps parents | We're having a huge party tonight because the peeps are out of town.

pseudo-__ not a real (noun), person who acts or looks like a (noun) but isn't | pseudo-Greek | pseudo-friend

Psych! Fooled you! | "Psych!" I said to Susan after tricking her into missing her final. [C339 chiefly teenagers: (an exclamation uttered when one has fooled or deceived another, meaning "I'm only kidding")]

psyched excited | I can't wait until the party tonight; I'm totally psyched. [C339; U87]

PSYCHED

psycho 1. weird, strange. 2. strange or weird person | It was a totally psycho party. No one was mingling or dancing or even having fun. | The guy in my history class is a real psycho. He closes his eyes and meditates through every lecture. [C340: 'crazy person']

P.T. see **pricktease**

< > marks words or usages that may be offensive to some or all speakers and that therefore should be used only with discretion; C = Chapman's *New Dictionary of American Slang;* U = previously collected UCLA slang. See the Introduction for more discussion. The Pronunciation Guide provides an explanation of the symbols used in phonetic transcriptions.

<pubehead> person with short, curly hair

puderhead person who doesn't meet one's expectations (pronounced [púdɚhɛd], like "ruder head") | My blind date was such a puderhead. He couldn't dance and didn't have an I.D. to drink. [?C340: pud 'penis' / Yiddish *puder* 'powder']

pull a __ to act like (name) | He pulled a Reagan and fell asleep during the meeting. [See also **pull a Fletch.**]

Pull a clue out of the clue bag! Think sensibly! Don't be so stupid!

pull a Fletch to do a con [<the movie *Fletch*. See also **pull a __.**]

pull an all-nighter to stay up all night | We pulled an all-nighter cramming for our linear programming final. [C340 teenagers: 'study all night']

pump 1. to make excited, turn on. 2. to have sex with. 3. ride on the back of a bike or scooter | That stripper at the party last night really pumped me. | Hey, Jane, since you have a two-seater how about giving me a pump? [(2): C342; C342: pumped up 'in a state of excited preparedness'. See also **Lick my love pump!**]

PUMP

puppy thing | after studying all night for his chemistry final, John said triumphantly, "I'm going to rip that puppy." [U84: puppies 'things']

<**pussy-whipped**> in love, infatuated, submissive, wrapped around (a girlfriend's) little finger (of a man) [C344: pussy-whipped 'dominated by one's wife or female lover'. See also **whipped.**]

putz idiot | Kevin drives on the freeway on a motorcycle without a helmet—what a putz. (pronounced [pʌts]—rhymes with "cuts") [<Yiddish *putz* 'penis'; C347: 'detestable person', 'ineffectual person']
➤ **putz around** to goof off [C347]

Qq

quacked see **That's quacked!**

Quarters drinking game in which quarters are bounced off the table into a glass | —Do you guys want to play Quarters? —No, we don't have enough beer.

queen <homosexual male> [C349 homosexuals]

__ **queen** female who is very (adjective), (verb)s a lot, or has a strong connection with (noun) | They call me the study queen because all I ever do is study. | She is a total fraternity queen. She spends all her time at fraternities. [See also __ **king.**]

MEN

QUEEN

< > marks words or usages that may be offensive to some or all speakers and that therefore should be used only with discretion; C = Chapman's *New Dictionary of American Slang*; U = previously collected UCLA slang. See the Introduction for more discussion. The Pronunciation Guide provides an explanation of the symbols used in phonetic transcriptions.

queer strange and unusual | I thought it was queer for my roommate to memorize my schedule, until I came home from class early and walked in on her and her boyfriend. [C349 1920s: 'homosexual'; U83: 'homosexual', 'strange, not likeable, weird'. See also **gay, homosexual.**]

Rr

rad / radical excellent, really great, fantastic | I had such a rad time there. I mean it was total fun. [<u>rad</u>ical; C351 teenagers; U83, 84, 87]

rag 1. unhappy, crabby, nasty, or *bitchy* female. 2. low blow, insult, burn [U83. See also **mung rag, on the rag.**]

RAG

➤ **rag on** to talk badly about; to nag [C352 late 1800s college students: 'to tease; banter disparagingly with'; U84: 'tease, pick on, be angry at']

rage 1. to have a wild, fantastic time. 2. to look good, be fashionable | That dress rages.
➤ **rager** person who rages; wild, fantastic party
➤ **raging** wild, fantastic | The party was raging. It was a rager.

raincoat condom

rake on to humiliate, criticize [See also **be raked.**]

ralph 1. to vomit. 2. penis [(1) C353 teenagers; (2) <Judy Blume's book *Forever*. See also **talk to Ralph on the big white phone**.]

__ **-rama** see __ **-o-rama**

rampage to go on a determined search through | As soon as the little girl I was baby-sitting for went to bed, I rampaged her family's refrigerator looking for snacks.

rancid 1. ugly. 2. bad-tasting | That dress with all those gross colors was really rancid.

random 1. bizarre. 2. ordinary. | That was a random test. [(2) U90]
- **Random Joe** some guy or other; any old guy | You mean you're just going to grovel with Random Joe?
- **random person** person who's not part of the usual group, outsider; ordinary person

rank disgusting, disagreeable, extremely ugly, *lame* | Her rank boy-friend has zits all over his face, greasy hair, and extra-large love handles.

RANK
- **rank on** to put down | He ranked on me.

rap pickup line

raped look see **just-raped look**

rat see **dorm rat, frat rat**

< > marks words or usages that may be offensive to some or all speakers and that therefore should be used only with discretion; C = Chapman's *New Dictionary of American Slang*; U = previously collected UCLA slang. See the Introduction for more discussion. The Pronunciation Guide provides an explanation of the symbols used in phonetic transcriptions.

ratfink to play a practical joke on [C354: 'treacherous and disgusting person']

RATFINK

<**ratfuck**> to break off a relationship with [C354 college students: 'unacceptable to conventional moral traditions']

raunchy disgusting, gross, ugly, tacky | That dress makes her look really raunchy. [C355 WWII Air Forces: 'sloppy, slovenly'; teenagers: 'inferior, cheap']

raw incredibly good, bold, untamed | Bobby's new B.M.W. is so raw! [U83: 'great']

rays see **bag rays**

real honest, unpretentious | She is the realest girl I have ever met. She doesn't wear makeup or try to act cute all the time. [See also **Be real!**]

ream 1. to treat unfairly. 2. to have anal sex with | The registrar reamed me again; I just got my study list and I am signed up for zero units. [C356; U84]

reek to stink, to be bad or unfair | I missed an A by one point—that really reeks.

reesch gross (pronounced [ríš], to rhyme with "leash") | I hate to see people pick their noses while they drive. That is so reesch!

REEK

remo stupid person, *nerd* (pronounced [rímo] —first syllable rhymes with "see," plus "Moe")

reverse gears to vomit | Watch out, everybody, I'm going to reverse gears!

ride bitch / sit bitch to ride in the middle of the backseat of a car | Please don't make me ride bitch again—I want shotgun!

ride shotgun / have shotgun to ride in the front passenger seat [C359 teenagers. See also **Shotgun!**]

RIDE SHOTGUN

ride the Buick to vomit | —What's wrong? —I have to go ride the Buick!!

ride the hobby horse to have sex | That ho rode the hobby horse all night.

ride the pine to sit on the bench during an athletic event, especially if one really wants to play

ridic ridiculous | That's ridic that you haven't started your twenty-page paper yet. [<ridiculous]

right see **Yeah, right!**

right in there see **be in there**

righteous see **do righteous**

RIP

rip 1. poor value for the money, rip-off. 2. to do very well, to be very successful

< > marks words or usages that may be offensive to some or all speakers and that therefore should be used only with discretion; C = Chapman's *New Dictionary of American Slang;* U = previously collected UCLA slang. See the Introduction for more discussion. The Pronunciation Guide provides an explanation of the symbols used in phonetic transcriptions.

| That sweater is such a rip at three hundred dollars. | Even though I had Bs on all the assignments in my English class, I ripped on the final and ended up with an A in the class. [(1) C360: rip off; (2) C360: 'a joy'; 'a try'. See also **let one rip.**]

rip on to talk about negatively; to nag; to *rag on* | When those two get together they totally rip on Jeff. [C360 black: 'to harass and insult']

ripped 1. having well-defined muscle tone. 2. drunk, intoxicated | The guy on the cover of *Flex* magazine was totally ripped. | I'm going to go downtown and get absolutely ripped. [C360 black: 'intoxicated'; U84 'drunk']

RIPPED

risk see **fashion risk, take a fashion risk**

road see **like five miles of bad road**

<roadwhore> girl who sleeps around, slut | Laura is a total roadwhore; she slept with three different guys in one week.

ROADWHORE

roast to embarrass in public [C361 fr early 1700s: 'make fun of, ridicule, insult']

rob to cut down or ridicule with a witty remark or comeback | Dude, you robbed her! What a comeback!

Rochambaud drinking game involving guessing which of several hand shapes someone will make (pronounced [rošæmbó], like "roe" plus "sham" plus "bow")

ROCHAMBAUD

rock 1. to fight with, to beat up. 2. piece of rock cocaine | He insulted my mother so I rocked him. [(1) U90; (2) C361]

Rock out! / Rock on! 1. Keep *partying*! 2. That's *cool*.

rock (someone's) world to have sex with (someone) | I'm going to rock her world.

Rocks for Jocks any easy geology class

rod penis [C362]

roll 1. to laugh hysterically. 2. to make (someone) laugh hysterically. 3. funny person | Eric is so funny—he's such a roll. [<rolling in the aisles; U84 'laugh hysterically']

ROLL

romp to have sex | Do you want to romp?

rough *cool* | That car is rough.

roust to tease, harass, attempt to humiliate | The bouncer rousted Joann when he slowly ripped up

< > marks words or usages that may be offensive to some or all speakers and that therefore should be used only with discretion; C = Chapman's *New Dictionary of American Slang*; U = previously collected UCLA slang. See the Introduction for more discussion. The Pronunciation Guide provides an explanation of the symbols used in phonetic transcriptions.

her fake I.D. at the front door. [C364 black: 'esp of police officers, to harass']

royal complete, big, *major* | That was a royal flop. [C364]

ROYAL

➤ **royally** completely, intensively | I blew that test royally. [U84]

rub see **Betty rub!**

rude 1. good, *cool, rad.* 2. gross, bad, unfair | Your brand-new convertible is so rude.

Rudeness! Rude! see **How rudeness!**

rug muncher see **carpet muncher**

rule to be the best | Our slang dictionary rules.

RULE

<rumpranger> homosexual male (pronounced [rʌmpræŋǰɚ], like "rump" plus "ranger")

run see **go on a ___ run**

rush to make a pass at; to confront; to go get | Let's go rush those shoes I saw yesterday at the store.

S s

___ 's balls are hot! (name) is drunk. | Mark's balls are hot. [<eyeballs]

sack to break up with, dump, treat (someone of the

opposite sex) badly [C367: 'discharge, dismiss']

sadistics statistics | I can't believe the amount of homework we get in sadistics.

SADISTICS

sadness see **Multiple sadness!**

salad see **do a fruit salad**

salami see **play hide the salami**

Sally person who is meticulous to the point of being anal-retentive or obsessive-compulsive, but in a cute way [<the movie *When Harry Met Sally*]

salt up to get in the way of or ruin (someone's) chances by saying the wrong thing or being a bother (usually used by the speaker about his or her own chances, with "me" as the object) | My little brother totally salted me up. He told my girlfriend I was out on a date with Pam.

sauced drunk, intoxicated | I was sauced after drinking a six-pack of beer. [C369: sauce 'liquor']

SAUCED

say see **Can you say "__"?**

scabs see **oozing scabs**

scam to make out knowing that it is meaningless, to look for someone to pick up, to flirt | They went to the bar to scam dudes. [C369 carnival: 'swindle,

< > marks words or usages that may be offensive to some or all speakers and that therefore should be used only with discretion; C = Chapman's *New Dictionary of American Slang*; U = previously collected UCLA slang. See the Introduction for more discussion. The Pronunciation Guide provides an explanation of the symbols used in phonetic transcriptions.

confidence game, fraud' (v); U84, 87]
➤ **scam on** to flirt with, to pick up on | Susie was scamming on Jay at the party last night. [U87]
➤ **scammer** person who scams [U83]

scarf 1. to eat (something) quickly. 2. to eat a lot quickly [C370; U83]
➤ **scarf on** to eat (something) quickly

scary unattractive, unpalatable, repulsive | When Mark came to class after only three hours of sleep, his friends said he looked scary.

SCARY

scene 1. plan; situation. 2. major, major field of interest | Here's the scene. I'll pick you up at six and then we will meet Jack at six-thirty. . . . | My scene is Theater Arts. [(2) C370: 'one's particular preference, activity, etc.']

scheize stuff (pronounced [šáyzə], like "shy" plus "zuh") | Dude, clear this scheize out of my room. It's in my way. [<German *Scheißen* or Yiddish *shayse* 'shit']
➤ **Scheize!** Shit!

SCHEIZE

schizo weird, strange, or bizarre | That man standing on his head in the street is schizo. [<schizo-phrenic]

scoob to eat, have some food (especially snacks) | Let's go scoob. I'm really starving to death! [<the

cartoon character Scooby Doo and his Scooby Snacks]

scoop on to pick up on, *hit on* | David thought that he was so sly, but I saw him trying to scoop on Nancy at the party.

scoot to ride a motor scooter

scope / scope out to evaluate, check out (a person or gathering, especially to look for attractive members of the opposite sex) | Jon was scoping the crowd at the party—he was scoped out by all the girls there. [C372: 'scope out'; U84: 'evaluate, search for']

SCOPE

score 1. to do well; to succeed (in a sexual relationship). 2. to get [C373: 'to succeed'; 'to do the sex act with'; students: 'to buy or get narcotics']
➤ **Score!** Good job! Congratulations! Way to go!

scream see **make (someone) scream**

screw / screw over to cause something bad to happen to, to be unfair to | My French professor screwed me over last quarter: she lowered my grade, claiming I was absent when I wasn't. [C374: 'to take advantage of, swindle, maltreat']

SCREW

➤ **screw around** to mess around, goof off
➤ **screw up** to do badly, make a mistake | I screwed up when I was honest with my girl-

---

< > marks words or usages that may be offensive to some or all speakers and that therefore should be used only with discretion; C = Chapman's *New Dictionary of American Slang*; U = previously collected UCLA slang. See the Introduction for more discussion. The Pronunciation Guide provides an explanation of the symbols used in phonetic transcriptions.

friend and told her that I got together with her best friend. [C375; U84]

➤ **screwed** 1. drunk, intoxicated. 2. messed up

➤ **screw-up** person who screws up; *loser*

scrounge 1. to take, borrow (something to which one's not entitled), to *mooch*. 2. scummy-looking person [C375 WWI British Army 'to acquire by such dubious ways as habitual borrowing, begging, foraging . . .'; scroungy 'inferior, wretched']

scrub 1. freshman. 2. slob. 3. to do badly, *mess up*. 4. to forget [(1, 2) C375 late 1800s: 'athlete who is not on the first or varsity team; a lowly substitute'; (4) C375: 'cancel or eliminate']

scrumptious see **get some scruptious**

scully person, boy, dude | What's up, scully?

scum gross-looking, vile, or unethical person; lowlife | I feel like such a scum. I haven't taken a shower all day. [See also **shower scum.**]

➤ **scumbucket** despicable person | Mark would steal candy from a baby, he's such a scumbucket! [C375: scumbag 'despicable person']

➤ **scummy** gross

➤ **scum-sucking pig** jerk [C376: scumsucking 'disgusting']

see see **Do you see skid marks on my forehead?, go to the doctor**

See ya! / C ya! Shut up! You're weird! Enough of that!

senioritis a loss of interest in academic aspects of school in anticipation of graduation | I've had senioritis since I was a sophomore.

serious real, genuine, *intense, major* | There's some serious partying going on tonight. [C378 black fr 1940s bop talk: 'excellent']

settle to calm down, settle down, relax (usually used as a command) | "Just settle!" Mary said to her younger brother, who was running around and yelling in the doctor's waiting room.

SETTLE

7 see **24-7**

seventh grader college student who has the maturity level and annoying characteristics of a seventh grader

Shacks! Shoot! Damn! | Shacks! I locked my keys in my car! [? <Shucks!]

shake see **the shake**

shake one's skirt to dance, especially, to go out dancing in a respectable nightclub (of a woman) | Terri, Cheri, and I are going to shake our skirts at the Golden Tails.

SHAKE ONE'S SKIRT

shake the dew off the lily see **knock the dew off the lily**

< > marks words or usages that may be offensive to some or all speakers and that therefore should be used only with discretion; C = Chapman's *New Dictionary of American Slang*; U = previously collected UCLA slang. See the Introduction for more discussion. The Pronunciation Guide provides an explanation of the symbols used in phonetic transcriptions.

sharp nice-looking (of clothes) | John, your pants and belt are sharp. [C380 jive talk: 'stylish']

Sheesh! (mild expletive used to show disbelief or disgust) | "For not being busy tonight, I sure made a lot of tips," said Marcie. "Sheesh!" Mark said, "I only made five dollars." [C381]

Sherlock see **No shit, Sherlock!**

shine to skip, *blow off* | She shined class yesterday because she had an important meeting to go to. [C382 teenagers fr black: 'to ignore, disregard, avoid'; U83: 'leave, leave (something)']

SHINE

➤ **Shine!** *N!* No way! | —Do you want to go to the movies with Melvin Belvin, his twin brother, and me? —Shine! [U84: 'forget it!']

shit 1. stuff, things. 2. a lot of, an undesirable amount of | —Hey, do you like heavy metal? —No, I'm not into shit like that. | I partied all week and now I have shit homework to do this weekend. [C383: 'nonsense'; 'one's possessions'. See also **Big shit! catch shit, chickenshit, have the shits, No shit! talk shit, the shit, up shit creek.**]

➤ **shit / shit bricks / shit in one's pants** to become overwhelmingly surprised, anxious, or nervous; to freak out; to worry excessively (past: shit, shitted, or shat, depending on the speaker; these expressions are often used with "almost") | I was shitting bricks when I found out I had to speak in front of the class. | I shit in my pants when I thought I lost my diamond ring. Thank goodness I found it!

➤ **Shit happens!** That's the way it goes!

Shit Lit American Popular Literature (English 115A) | In Shit Lit we are reading *Wanderlust* and *Hondo.*

shitfaced drunk, intoxicated | John got really shitfaced at a party last night. He said he had twelve beers.

Shitlaw! Fuck! Damn! | Shitlaw! I just failed my second midterm in this class.

shitlist unwritten list of people or things that one does not like | That girl Tracy is such a bitch. She's on my shitlist. | Lima beans have been on Ben's shitlist ever since he was a kid. [C384: 'one's fancied or real list of persons who are hated']

SHITLIST

shmuck fool, idiot, failure, jerk | Ken was pulled over on the freeway for driving a hundred miles an hour. He then asked the officer why he was pulled over. What a shmuck! [<Yiddish *shmuck* 'penis'; C372: 'detestable person']

Shock a broe! / Shock a brew! Have a beer! (broe pronounced [bró], to rhyme with "low") [<Ha-

waiian Pidgin *shaka brah* 'right on, brother']

shoot hoop / shoot hoops / shoot some hoop / shoot some hoops / play hoops to play basketball | We're gonna shoot some hoop after class today.

shop / shopping see **window shop**

shotgun 1. to drink a full can of beer all at one time (especially from a hole poked in the bottom). 2. to drink (a full can of beer) all at one time (especially from a hole poked in the bottom). | I shotgunned. | He shotgunned a beer. [See also **ride shotgun.**]

➤ **Shotgun!** I get the front passenger seat (in a car)! Dibs on the front passenger seat!

shower scum / pond scum / bathtub scum slime, filth | Lloyd is such shower scum. He's got three girlfriends, and each thinks she's the only one in his life.

shower spank see **spank**

shred to do well on, do well with, conquer | He's a great surfer; he really shredded that wave, didn't he? [U87]

shredded drunk, intoxicated

Shut up! Are you serious? No way! Not even! | —I saw Bill Cosby on campus—he even said hi to me. —Shut up!

sick bad, of poor quality; strange; gross; stupid,

uncool | I have the sickest classes this quarter; they're all early in the morning. [C359 1950s: 'gruesome, morbid, mentally unhealthy']

➤ **sick and wrong** horrible, disgusting, unthinkable (usually pronounced [sɪkənrá::ŋ:g], like "sickenwrooonnng," with the o and the n lengthened and the g sounded—often used as an exclamation) | You want to set me up with him. . . . Sick and wrong! Just because I don't have a date doesn't mean I'm desperate.

simp fool, imbecile | The simp at the podium didn't realize his fly was open during the entire speech. [C390]

single see **be single**

sit shotgun see **ride shotgun**

SIMP

sixer six-pack of beer | I bought two sixers for the game.

skag ugly girl; slutty-looking girl; *ho* | Not only is Jeannette buttly, by the way she flirts, it's obvious she's a skag, too. [C392 black fr 1920s: 'unattractive woman']

➤ **skaggy** having the characteristics of a skag

SKAG

skank 1. cheap-looking, ugly, unprincipled, snooty, or condescending girl, *bitch.* 2. good-

< > marks words or usages that may be offensive to some or all speakers and that therefore should be used only with discretion; C = Chapman's *New Dictionary of American Slang;* U = previously collected UCLA slang. See the Introduction for more discussion. The Pronunciation Guide provides an explanation of the symbols used in phonetic transcriptions.

looking girl | My chemistry lab partner thinks she's too hot to give me any help with experiments—she's a total skank. [C392 black: 'an unattractive woman, a malodorous woman']

➤ **skanky** 1. cheap-looking, ugly, unprincipled (of a girl). 2. good-looking (of a girl) [C392 teenagers fr black: 'nasty, repellent'. See also **stank.**]

➤ **skanky box** slutty woman | She's such a skanky box, she'll probably never get married.

Skate or die! see **Thrash or die!**

skate rat person who skateboards a lot or is very good at skateboarding | Your little brother's such a cute little skate rat. But don't you ever get tired of him draining your pool to skate in it?

skeezer promiscuous woman, slut, *ho* | That skeezer has slept with every man in the room.

sketch 1. to be sketchy, feel sketchy. 2. person who is sketchy. 3. close call | We almost got hit—what a sketch.

➤ **sketch out** to be paranoid; to have a bad trip, *freak out* | He's totally sketching out—he thinks everyone is out to get him.

SKETCH

➤ **sketched** bad, weird

➤ **sketchy** unsure, unstable, confused; jittery; strange, *hairy* | Something really sketchy happened last Halloween. [U84: 'ugly, hard to deal with, disagreeable']

skid marks see **Do you see skid marks on my forehead?**

skin flute see **play the skin flute**

skip on to beat it, go away (*skips on, *skipped on, *skipping on) | After Simon had been hanging around for twenty minutes, flirting, several of the girls asked him to skip on. [C393 middle 1800s: skip 'to depart hastily']

SKIP ON

skirt see **shake one's skirt**

slag <ugly or slutty-looking girl> [?C392 black 1920s: skag 'unattractive woman'. See also **skank.**]
➤ **slagheap** <ugly or slutty-looking girl>

slam 1. to beat badly. 2. to have sex. 3. to have sex with. 4. to drink quickly | Well, did you slam her, Jon? | He slammed two beers and then went out on his date.
➤ **slammed** drunk, intoxicated

slapped with an ugly stick see **be beat with an ugly stick**

slaughtered drunk, intoxicated

sleazebag low-down, *scummy* person, jerk, *loser* | Ronnie's a total sleazebag; he spits on people when he talks to them. [C395; U84].

< > marks words or usages that may be offensive to some or all speakers and that therefore should be used only with discretion; C = Chapman's *New Dictionary of American Slang;* U = previously collected UCLA slang. See the Introduction for more discussion. The Pronunciation Guide provides an explanation of the symbols used in phonetic transcriptions.

sleeper boring class | If the professor has no enthusiasm, the class can become a total sleeper.

sleestak sleazy girl (pronounced [slístæk], like "slee" plus "stack") | There were so many sleestaks at the party that I felt really out of place, so I left. [<creature on "Land of the Lost"]

slime filth, *shower scum* (term applied to a disgusting male, especially one who has hurt a female emotionally in a relationship)

<**slip (someone) the hot beef injection**> / <**give (someone) the hot beef injection**> to have sex with (a female) | Mark is so obnoxious! He asked me if my boyfriend has ever slipped me the hot beef injection. [<*The Breakfast Club*]

sloppy see **get sloppy**

sloshed drunk, intoxicated | After I drank four wine coolers, two shots of vodka, and three beers, I was so sloshed, I could barely stand up. [C397]

sloth / slug extremely lazy person, who may not even get out of bed all day [See also **maggot.**]

SLOTH

smack 1. intelligent, overachieving student; *geek.* 2. nonsense, gibberish | Lorraine gets straight As; she's such a smack. [<the sound of a kiss. See also **kiss ass, talk shit.**]

smart see **book smart**

smashed 1. drunk, intoxicated. 2. really tired | I got smashed last night and I'm hating life this morning. [C399]

smile see **working man's smile**

Smiley name for a guy with a *working man's smile*

Smith see **Mr. Smith**

smoke to beat (in competition) | Our football team's going to smoke the competition this year. [See also **blow smoke up (someone's) ass.**]

smoke a bowl / smoke a toke to smoke marijuana | C'mon, dude, let's smoke a bowl. [C42: bowl 'marijuana'; C441; toke 'a puff or drag at a . . . marijuana cigarette']

snack / treat particle of a substance in an unexpected or incorrect place | I walked into the bathroom and there was a snack on the toilet.

snag to take, to steal | When we left the store, Jean told me she had snagged three bottles of nail polish.

SNAG nice guy (like someone on "thirtysomething" who is able to cry and takes his dates to trendy restaurants [<u>s</u>ensitive <u>n</u>ew-<u>age</u> <u>g</u>uy]

snake 1. to steal (something). 2. to cheat (someone), to get ahead of (someone) unfairly. 3. penis | I snaked that

SNAKE

parking place before the other guy got to it.

snotnose conceited, spoiled, irritating, or immature person | That sixteen-year-old with the Jag is probably a real snotnose. [C402: 'importunate upstart']

➤ **snotnosed** conceited, spoiled, irritating, or immature | Beverly Hills kids are snotnosed because they drive B.M.W.s.

So Cool Southern California | He's from So Cool. [See also **No Cool.**]

so fast gladly | Billy Idol? He's my favorite singer. I'll go to his concert so fast.

soaked drunk, intoxicated [C402 middle 1700s]

Sob! Shoot! Damn! | Your date canceled on you at the last minute and didn't give you a reason? Sob!

sober see **Easy!**

soc person with a superficial personality who is known for participating in a lot of social activities (usually, a girl) (pronounced [sóš], like "soshe"; plural: **soshes**) | She was such a soc in high school, I'm not surprised that she's rushing the most popular sorority. [C403 teenagers: 'social climber']

S.O.L. out of luck, in an unfortunate situation | Marcie wanted a car for Christmas; when she didn't receive it, Tracy said, "You're S.O.L." [<shit out of luck; C404 esp WWI armed forces: 'ruined']

solid very good, without flaw | That banner is really solid. I bet you it will win something. [C404 jive talk fr 1930s]

some see **get some, get some scrumptious, have some __, want some,** or see word following **some** in a given expression

SOLID

sorority incredibly superficial-looking (of a girl: usually, having bleached blond hair, lots of makeup, and a hair bow) | She was so sorority! [See also **Suzy Sorority.**]
> - **sorority girl** incredibly superficial-looking girl (usually with bleached blond hair, lots of makeup, and a bow in her hair)

sorrow overrun with sorority girls | This party is sorrow, let's bail! [<sorority row]

space to let one's mind wander, to daydream | I really need to study, but I keep spacing. [C406 teenagers; U84: 'someone whose mind is always wandering']
> - **space cadet / space case** *airhead* [C406: space cadet 'mad or eccentric person'; U84]
> - **space out** to be semiconscious, act as if one is under the influence of drugs, act out of touch with what's going on around one [C404 teenagers: 'daydream . . . not attend to what one is doing']
> - **spaced / spaced out** 1. dazed; out of touch

> marks words or usages that may be offensive to some or all speakers and that therefore ould be used only with discretion; C = Chapman's *New Dictionary of American Slang;* U = eviously collected UCLA slang. See the Introduction for more discussion. The Pronunciation uide provides an explanation of the symbols used in phonetic transcriptions.

with what is going on around one. 2. under the influence of a drug | Jeff is always taking drugs. Every time I see him, he's spaced out on something different. [C404, 406; U83 'acting or seeming odd or inappropriate']

➤ **spacy** out of touch with reality, *airheaded* [C404–05: 'in a daze'; 'crazy or eccentric']

spank 1. to beat badly (in competition). 2. to goof off | My opponent was terrible. I spanked him.

➤ **spank / shower spank** to masturbate (of a male) | It's not cool to spank in public.   SPANK

spaz person who is hyper or *spazzy* [<spastic; C407 esp teenagers fr 1960s: 'strange or stupid person'; U83: 'frantic reaction', spaz out 'react frantically']

➤ **spaz out** to *freak out*

➤ **spazzy** energetically weird, hyper | The professor was so spazzy that the class got frightened. [C407 teenagers fr 1960s: 'stupid']

special see **Isn't that special!**

Special K pinches bulges of extra fat around the waist [<the "you can't pinch an inch" Special K commercial]

<sped> slow, stupid person | Larry, don't be such a sped—you know the answer. [<special education]

SPECIAL K PINCHES

spew 1. to ejaculate. 2. semen. 3. to vomit | Don't spew on me, Mark! | Did you see Kerry after she did all those vodka shots? She spewed all over her boyfriend's lap!

spiders see **barking spiders**

spikes shoes (any kind, for men or women) | Allen, that's a real trendy outfit. Are those new spikes?

SPIKES

spill to fall | He threw away his skateboard the first time he spilled.

spin (someone's) wheels to excite (someone, especially in a sexual sense) | He really spins my wheels. [C408: spin one's wheels 'waste time']

splooge 1. to ejaculate. 2. semen (pronounced [splúǰ]—rhymes with "huge") | Last night I accidentally got splooge on the wall. [See also **spoo, spooch.**]

sponge person who drinks a lot [C409]

spoo sperm | Men can make a lot of money selling their spoo to local spoo banks. [See also **splooge, spooch.**]

spooch 1. to ejaculate. 2. semen (pronounced [spúč]—rhymes with "pooch") [See also **splooge, spoo.**]

< > marks words or usages that may be offensive to some or all speakers and that therefore should be used only with discretion; C = Chapman's *New Dictionary of American Slang;* U = previously collected UCLA slang. See the Introduction for more discussion. The Pronunciation Guide provides an explanation of the symbols used in phonetic transcriptions.

sport 1. to give. 2. to wear | The cops confiscated all my booze on the way over here. Could you sport me a beer?

➤ **sport a woody** to have an erection

➤ **sporting** looking good | In his double-breasted suit, Josh was really sporting.

➤ **sporty** cool-looking

spouse really serious boyfriend or girl-friend

SPORT

sprung on see **be sprung on**

square (someone's) circle to have sex with (someone) | She dragged him into her room and squared his circle.

squeeze 1. accidental, lucky. 2. shoddy, of poor quality | That goal was really squeeze; you shouldn't get that point at all. | Nobody will wear that T-shirt 'cause it's got such a squeeze design.

squid jerk, *nerd* [U83: 'short person, wimp']

squirt see **Hershey squirt**

stank ugly | She's so stank that I can't even look at her. [U83: stanky 'cute, promiscuous'; stanky tuna 'cute and/or promiscuous female'; 87: stanky 'revolting'. See also **skank, skanky.**]

SQUID

stellar really great, fantastic | She was in some silky dress, her hair was down, and she generally looked stellar.

stewed in trouble, *screwed*

stick 1. to have sex with (of a male; past: sticked).
2. to hit (past: stuck) | He totally sticked her after
the party. [See also **be beat with an ugly stick,
beat (someone) with an ugly stick.**]

stoked excited, happy (often as a result of good
luck), high on life | This biology class seems really
good. I'm so stoked that I got into it. [C417 teenagers; U83 'embarrassed', 86, 87]
➤ **stoke up** to please | The news about Eric
stoked up the team.
➤ **Stoke me! / Stoke me up!** That's *cool*! That
makes me so happy!

stomp (someone's) buzz see **kill (someone's)
buzz, buzzkill**

stoned drunk, intoxicated; under the
influence of drugs [C418; U84]
➤ **stoner** person who looks as
though he or she uses drugs a lot;
person who uses drugs, or who
has the glassy-eyed, out-of-it look of one who
uses drugs | Everyone at the Cure concert was
dancing except the stoners, who just sat and
stared at the stage. [C418: 'intoxicated or stu-
porous person']

STONED

<> marks words or usages that may be offensive to some or all speakers and that therefore
should be used only with discretion; C = Chapman's *New Dictionary of American Slang;* U =
previously collected UCLA slang. See the Introduction for more discussion. The Pronunciation
Guide provides an explanation of the symbols used in phonetic transcriptions.

strawberry slut, promiscuous woman (especially, one who sleeps around in order to get free drugs)

stress to worry a lot, get nervous, get performance anxiety | Janice began to stress about her two midterms the night before she had to take them. [U90: stress out]

> **stress case** extremely stressed person, person that is constantly feeling stressed | Jill is a total stress case. She's bitten all her nails down to her cuticles worrying about her exam.
> STRESS

stressmonger / stressmonster an extremely stressed person, person who is constantly feeling stressed | Relax, Mary, you'll pass the test, you studied all weekend. Stop being such a stressmonster! [U87: stress-monger]

stroke 1. to masturbate. 2. to con, deceive [C420]

strumpet sleazy girl, unattractive girl | Look at that girl over there. Her skirt is so short that I can see her underwear, and you can tell she's not even wearing a bra. What a strumpet!

stud 1. person who has done something outstanding; cool, good-looking, or popular person; guy who is successful with a lot of girls. 2. conceited person | Everyone knows Mike, he's the total stud of his class. [C421: 'attractive man']

STUD

> **stud out** to accomplish something great, to do well (usually used about a past event) | When

Mary announced that she got the lead role in a new movie, her friend exclaimed, "That's wonderful! You really studded out!"

➤ **studette** female stud (in all senses); girl who gets a guy she wants

➤ **studly** *cool* (sometimes, too cool) | Jenny, look at all of the studly guys in here. I would happily go out with any of them.

➤ **studmuffin** strong, muscular person; cute person; achiever, go-getter | Number forty-four of the football team is such a studmuffin. | Suzy is such a studmuffin. No one else could have juggled a job, an internship, and a high G.P.A. [U90: studmuffin / muffin]

➤ **studola** see __-ola

study see **powerstudy**

stupid crazy | He's acting stupid on us.

styling doing good, looking good | You got an A in physics! You're styling! [C421 black: style 'to act or play in a showy, flamboyant way' (pres part); U84, 87]

subhuman 1. stupid, socially unacceptable, gross. 2. stupid, gross, or socially unacceptable person | When Peter gets drunk, he acts really subhuman. | That guy is a subhuman—you can tell by the ugly clothes he wears and the way he acts.

SUBHUMAN

< > marks words or usages that may be offensive to some or all speakers and that therefore should be used only with discretion; C = Chapman's *New Dictionary of American Slang*; U = previously collected UCLA slang. See the Introduction for more discussion. The Pronunciation Guide provides an explanation of the symbols used in phonetic transcriptions.

submarine tampon

suck to be bad, to be a terrible situation | "It sucks that I have eight o'clock classes every day of the week," Bob said. [C422: 'to be disgusting or extremely reprehensible; be of wretched quality'; U83, 84, 87. See also **sucky.**]

SUCK

Suck! Fuck! Darn! Shoot!

suck it easy to take it easy, relax | After working all day I was sucking it easy on the couch.

➤ **suck it up** to deal with it, tolerate it, endure a problem; to live it up, get the most out of something | I don't care if you're tired of running, and I don't care how much pain you're in. Just suck it up! [C422: 'to become serious, stop dallying or loafing']

suck up to try to win favor

➤ **suck up to** to try desperately to win the favor of (usually with ulterior motives) [C422 middle 1800s British: 'to flatter and cajole someone; curry favor with someone']

➤ **sucker** one who sucks up

sucky awful | That was the suckiest test I've ever taken. It was even suckier than the one my sucky Astronomy teacher gave last quarter. [<suck + y]

Surf or die! (belittling comment used about someone who seems obsessed with surfing) [See also **Thrash or die!**]

Suzy Sorority someone who belongs to a sorority [See also **Tina Tridelt.**]

sweet 1. great, very appealing (often, of a car). 2. effeminate | That car is so sweet, but I don't think that I can afford it. [U83, 87: 'great, excellent, cool']

swellhead arrogant person, stuck-up person, conceited person | Judy thinks she is so beautiful and so wonderful for winning the beauty pageant. She is such a swellhead. [C425]

SWELLHEAD

swoon to shiver, gasp, become lightheaded just by looking at a male who looks good | I saw Scott across the crowded room and swooned like I never had before.
➤ **Swoon!** (exclamation used on noticing a new attractive man)

swoop on 1. to come on to, make a pass at (a member of the opposite sex). 2. to pass (vehicles or people) | He fully swooped on her and they ended up mashing. | Tanya swooped on everyone in the track meet on Saturday.
➤ **Swoop!** (exclamation used about swooping on) | On the way to the Boingo concert I drove in the emergency lane and swooped on thirty cars. As I drove by I said, "Swoop!"

< > marks words or usages that may be offensive to some or all speakers and that therefore should be used only with discretion; C = Chapman's *New Dictionary of American Slang;* U = previously collected UCLA slang. See the Introduction for more discussion. The Pronunciation Guide provides an explanation of the symbols used in phonetic transcriptions.

Tt

tacky tasteless, tactless, *uncool* | Cheryl wore that blue sweater twice and then returned it to the department store for a refund. That's so tacky! | Minutes after he found out about a girl who committed suicide, John told jokes about dying. How tacky! [C427 late 1800s southern: 'inferior, shabby, vulgar'; U83: 'tasteless']

<**tail gunner**> male homosexual [C427 fr 1300s: tail 'the buttocks']

take a chill pill to calm down, not get upset, not *stress out* | This class is not as difficult as you think, Glenn, so take a chill pill. [See also **chill out.**]

take a dip to chew tobacco | C'mon, dude, let's take a dip. [C103: dip]

take a fashion risk to dress unattractively [See also **fashion risk.**]

➤ **take a fashion risk with** to look unattractive in | She's taking a fashion risk with that skirt.

Take a Midol! Stop being so difficult! Calm down! (used to either males or females) | You don't have to get so upset, Stephanie, take a Midol.

Take a picture! Stop staring! | Take a picture! You have been looking at me for an hour!

take cuts to get in front of someone in a

TAKE A PICTURE!

line (either sneakily, or because someone lets one in) [See also **give (someone) cuts, have cuts.**]

Take it down a thousand! Relax! Calm down! | Julie, take it down a thousand! Just because you got a C on your chemistry test doesn't mean it's the end of the world.

Take it easy! Calm down! Goodbye for now! (parting phrase) | —Well, I'll see you later. —Yeah, take it easy. [C429. See also **Easy!**]

Take it on! *Go for it!*

take the zero to turn down an offer, to pass something up | —Do you want to order a pizza tonight? —No, I'll take the zero.

talk head to talk in a negative way | Every time I talk to Charlie he's always talking head.

talk shit / talk smack to talk (about someone) in a negative way; to talk big; to talk about nothing | Laura was really talking shit about him behind his back.

talk to Ralph on the big white phone to vomit into the toilet | —What's he doing? —Oh, he's just in the bathroom talking to Ralph on the big white phone. [C431: talk to the big white phone 'vomit into the toilet bowl'. See also **ralph.**]

< > marks words or usages that may be offensive to some or all speakers and that therefore should be used only with discretion; C = Chapman's *New Dictionary of American Slang*; U = previously collected UCLA slang. See the Introduction for more discussion. The Pronunciation Guide provides an explanation of the symbols used in phonetic transcriptions.

talk to the mike <to perform oral sex (on a male)> | The guy at the party told me to talk to the mike, so I slapped him across the face.

talking with see **be talking with**

tank time time to have a drink | "I think it's tank time," said Mark at the start of "Monday Night Football." [See also **Miller time.**]

tanka large soft drink (pronounced [tǽŋkə], to rhyme with "Sanka") | We need to go to 7-11 and get tankas.

tanked drunk, intoxicated [C431 late 1800s]

taste / tasty very good, nice looking, enviable (especially, of cars) | His Porsche is way tasty. | He bought the most taste car.

TANKED

tatas see **bodacious tatas**

tater see **whack the tater**

tattered drunk, intoxicated

team dressing or acting in a style typical of some easily identifiable group | Wearing your visor backwards and your Adidas sandals with socks is just too team, bro.

TEAM

➤ **team** ___ dressing or acting in the style that epitomizes the (noun / adjective) group, whether one is a member of that group or not | team cycling | team Hollywood | team stupid

team Xerox 1. to cheat. 2. act of cheating. 3. copied, done as a result of cheating | We were team Xeroxing it on the math exam because none of us had studied. | That test was a team Xerox effort. We all helped each other. | We pulled a team Xerox. I hope no one saw us.

tease see **dicktease, pricktease**

teats breasts | The only reason Jeff goes out with her is because he's obsessed with her teats.

technicolor yawn vomit; the act of vomiting | He went running to the bathroom yelling, "Get out of my way or you're going to see a technicolor yawn." [C433 teenagers]

Texas hair see **big hair**

T.F.A. great | Your new Porsche is T.F.A. [<totally fucking awesome]

thang thing | That girl is such a wild thang. | What's your weekend thang? We're going to the movies.

that see **Bag that!**

That's cool! Everything is fine! O.K. [U84: it's cool]

THAT'S COOL!

< > marks words or usages that may be offensive to some or all speakers and that therefore should be used only with discretion; C = Chapman's *New Dictionary of American Slang*; U = previously collected UCLA slang. See the Introduction for more discussion. The Pronunciation Guide provides an explanation of the symbols used in phonetic transcriptions.

That's quacked! That's unfair!

the big X one's menstrual period | I couldn't wear white pants because I was on the big X. [<X marked on a calendar]

the crib home | I'll see you later, I'm going to kick it at the crib. [C88 teen-agers: crib 'home']

THE CRIB

<the fuck> the hell | What the fuck are you talking about?

<the fuck eye> a flirtatious look, the eye [See also **fuck-me eyes.**]

the kind / da kine the best | Fuck, dude, this pot is the kind. [C246 teen-agers: the kind; U84]

THE FUCK EYE

the Row fraternity or sorority row | There are so many parties on the Row tonight, I can't decide which one to go to.

the shake an undesirable person | She's the shake. I wouldn't go out with her if she paid me.

the shit someone or something important or *cool* | He thinks he is the shit.

the wild thing sex, sexual intercourse [See also **do the deed.**]

there see **be in there, be out of there, be there**

thesaurus see **walking dictionary**

thing see **do the deed, thang, the wild thing**

third leg penis [C277]

___ this! Shut up! Leave me alone! (used in response to a remark or suggestion, repeating a word [usually the verb] from it) | —Let's go grab a hamburger at the Cooperage! —Grab this! / Hamburger this! Don't you know I'm on a diet?

thousand see **Take it down a thousand!**

thrash to wreck, *mess up* | I was so angry because I lent my car to my friend and she thrashed it. [See also **trash**.]

THRASH

➤ **thrash on** to criticize | She thrashed on her boyfriend because he was looking at other girls.

Thrash or die! / Skate or die! (belittling comment used about someone who seems obsessed with skateboarding) [See also **Surf or die!**]

thrashed 1. worn out, in bad condition; very bad. 2. drunk, intoxicated | My suede shoes were thrashed after I wore them in the rain. | His grades are going to be thrashed after this test! | After eight beers he was totally thrashed. [U84, 87: 'worn out'. See also **trashed**.]

thrasher 1. a destructive person. 2. a skateboarder. 3. wild or destructive party. 4. wild (of a party) | That was a thrasher party.

Three Man drinking game played with dice

throg to drink | When I get to Bea's party, I'm gonna throg until I can't see.

THRASHER

throw attitude / throw tude / give attitude / give tude to act in a rude, snobbish, or angry manner | The professor asked me to leave because I was throwing tude. [See also **attitude.**]

THROW ATTITUDE

throw down to instigate something, to say something critical or provocative; to fight | Sandy really threw down in her speech and let everyone know what she has been thinking. [C437: 'to threaten or challenge']

throw (someone) attitude / throw (someone) tude / give (someone) attitude / give (someone) tude to act in a rude, snobbish, or angry manner to | We didn't like the way the waitress was treating us, so we threw her attitude. [See also **throw attitude.**]

throw the dagger / throw one's dagger to have sex with someone (of a man) | Did you throw your dagger last night?

throw tude see **throw attitude**

thumber constant borrower, *mooch* | Barbara is such a thumber—she is always borrowing money.

thump 1. to have sex with. 2. to have sex

Thumper drinking game played by thumping on the table, in which each player has a different made-up name or gesture

THUMPER

thunder to do well | You're so well prepared— you're gonna thunder on the exam.

ticking see **be ticking**

tiger see **Easy!**

tight 1. mean, nasty, strict. 2. close (of friends). 3. good-looking. 4. stingy. 5. very toned physically | That was really tight of your mom to kick you out of the house. [C438 early 1800s: 'parsimonious'; 'close, sympathetic'; U84; 'insensitive, not nice', 'very toned physically (of a female)']

tight-ass person who is uptight and overly concerned with rules or social responsibility | The Parking Service is a bunch of tight-asses. [C438: 'tense and morally rigid person']

TIGHT-ASS

➤ **tight-assed** uptight, rigidly conforming to regulations; frigid [C438: 'tense; overly formal'; U84]

< > marks words or usages that may be offensive to some or all speakers and that therefore should be used only with discretion; C = Chapman's *New Dictionary of American Slang;* U = previously collected UCLA slang. See the Introduction for more discussion. The Pronunciation Guide provides an explanation of the symbols used in phonetic transcriptions.

time see **big time, major time, Miller time, tank time**

Tina Tridelt someone female who is incredibly superficial-looking or -acting, who may or may not be a sorority member [See also **Suzy Sorority.**]

to the curb ugly, no good, *scummy* | That's a to the curb dress. | Johnny, you're to the curb. [See also **be to the curb.**]

toasted slightly intoxicated, *buzzed*; really drunk | They were toasted after a couple of margaritas.

TOASTED

toes see **frito toes**

together see **get together**

toke see **Cap'n Toke, smoke a bowl**

tonsil hockey see **play tonsil hockey**

toot 1. to pass gas, fart. 2. cocaine | —What's that smell? —Oh, Andrea tooted again.

TOOT

torqued drunk, intoxicated

toss 1. to vomit. 2. to flirt out of a sense of desperation, to throw oneself at someone | After he drank too much and danced too much, no one was surprised that he tossed except him. | Christy is going to get a bad reputation if she keeps tossing at those fraternity parties.

➤ **toss one's cookies** to vomit | He tossed his cookies after the tequila party. [C385]

total 1. complete, absolute. 2. totally | I was total hungry.
➤ **totally** very, completely, really [U83, 84, 87]
➤ **Totally!** Yeah! Really!

tough nice-looking (usually, of clothing or accessories) | He's got on a tough suit. [C444 cool talk & students fr 1960s: 'excellent']

TOUGH

trap girl who demonstrates interest in a male, then abruptly becomes uninterested; tease | We went out to lunch and she kissed me, and now she ignores me—what a trap!

trash to destroy | He got totally blitzed and trashed the whole upstairs. [C445 late 1960s. See also **thrash.**]
➤ **trashed** 1. totally exhausted. 2. drunk, intoxicated | I was so trashed after cramming for midterms all night. | Mark got so trashed at the frat party last night, he lost his balance and fell down the stairs. [U87: 'drunk']

treat cute girl | Hey, Bob, let's go dancing and pick up on some treats. [See also **snack.**]

tree girl who is six feet or taller | A girl who is six feet tall who's a virgin would be a cherry tree! [See also **nail Jell-O to a tree**]

< > marks words or usages that may be offensive to some or all speakers and that therefore should be used only with discretion; C = Chapman's *New Dictionary of American Slang;* U = previously collected UCLA slang. See the Introduction for more discussion. The Pronunciation Guide provides an explanation of the symbols used in phonetic transcriptions.

trendy faddish (of a person or clothing); fashionable (of a restaurant, for instance)
- ➤ **trendoid / trendy** person who is slavishly devoted to current trends | Look at Jack's new boots. He's such a trendoid, he bought them after a few guys in his fraternity bought some.

trick neat, interesting | I love that dress in the window; it's so trick.

Tridelt see **Tina Tridelt**

trim see **get some trim**

trip 1. to act inappropriately, react unexpectedly; to act crazy or weird, *freak out*. 2. person who's funny or weird | I tripped when I found out the man I was dating was actually a woman. [C446 narcotics & students fr 1970s: 'a psychedelic narcotics experience' (v); U83: 'bizarre, strange person', 'have one's mind wander off'. See also **What a trip!**]

TRICK

troll 1. <ugly girl>. 2. girl under six feet tall (when contrasted with a very tall one). 3. lecherous middle-aged or older man | Mary's fat and her face looks like a bird just sat on it. What a troll! [U84: 'someone who hangs around a group of people hoping to be picked up']

trollop loose girl, girl who sleeps around | Becky is a total trollop. She has been with so many guys this quarter that I can't even count them on both hands.

trouser trout penis

truck 1. person who runs or moves slowly. 2. to move slowly | He's such a truck; he's the slowest person on the team. | How are we ever going to be on time if you truck? [C447: 'carry; haul; drag']

TROUSER TROUT

try to front / want to front to say negative things about people, be confrontational | Why do you want to front?

<**tubesteak of love**> penis [C447: tube steak 'frankfurter'. See also **weenie.**]

tude see **attitude, throw attitude, throw (someone) attitude**

turbobitch crabby, *bitchy* female [See also **turboslut.**]

turboslut very sleazy girl | Julie is a turboslut. [See also **turbobitch, hyperdrive whore.**]

twack twelve-pack (of beer) | I think if anyone drank a twack they would be rather toasted. [<twelve-pack]

tweak to hurt, damage | I totally tweaked my ankle in aerobics class. [U90]
➤ **tweak / tweak out** to go weird; to *freak out* | My hair is totally tweaking out.

< > marks words or usages that may be offensive to some or all speakers and that therefore should be used only with discretion; C = Chapman's *New Dictionary of American Slang*; U = previously collected UCLA slang. See the Introduction for more discussion. The Pronunciation Guide provides an explanation of the symbols used in phonetic transcriptions.

➤ **tweaked** 1. crazy. 2. drunk, intoxicated. 3. not working right, *messed up,* strange. 4. tired. 5. *wired* | Julie is tweaked—first she says she loves Doug and then she fully grovels with Bill. [See also **twig out.**]

➤ **tweaked out** tired [U84]

24-7 all the time, every hour of every day | I had to study 24-7 for that exam.

twig skinny person [See also **stick.**]

twig out to become overwhelmingly anxious, to *freak out* | I twigged out in class today when I found out our midterm will be held on Wednesday and not sometime next week. [See also **tweak out.**]

TWIG OUT

twisted 1. drunk, intoxicated. 2. weird, crazy, funny | Having a history question on our chem test was so twisted.

twit fool, *lame* person, *loser* | He's such a twit; he always crank-calls me! [C450 1920s British: 'trivial idiot']

➤ **twitty** having the characteristics of a twit

two bagger / double bagger ugly person (so ugly you need to put one bag over his or her head and one over yours just in case his or hers rips) [C450. See also **one bagger.**]

U u

U. see **Pretty People U.**

ugly see **be beat with an ugly stick, beat (someone) with an ugly stick, coyote ugly, fugly, mufugly**

U.M.S. undesirable change in mood, for no particular reason [<ugly mood swing]

uncool not good, unfair, tactless, showing poor social judgment | It was very uncool of the professor to tell us about the midterm the day before we had to take it. [C451]

up shit creek / up the creek / up shit's creek in a bad or troublesome situation from which there is no easy escape | Oh my God, the computer just erased my paper and it's due in half an hour. I'm up shit creek. [C453]

up the butt to the degree of being excessive, unending, or overwhelming | What with classes in microbiology, chemistry, and history, I've got homework up the butt. [C452: up the kazoo; 453: up the ass. See also **up the ying yang.**]

UP THE BUTT

up the creek see **up shit creek**

up the ying yang in superabundance, to excess |

< > marks words or usages that may be offensive to some or all speakers and that therefore should be used only with discretion; C = Chapman's *New Dictionary of American Slang;* U = previously collected UCLA slang. See the Introduction for more discussion. The Pronunciation Guide provides an explanation of the symbols used in phonetic transcriptions.

Because I didn't study at all this weekend, I now have homework up the ying yang. [C481: ying-yang 'the anus'. See also **up the butt, yang yang.**]

up to no good see **be up to no good**

U.S.A. see __ **-ville, U.S.A.**

Vv

vacuum person who eats very fast, person who eats anything in sight | When Andrea spilled her chips, she ate them off the ground. What a vacuum!

vamos see **Let's vamos!**

V.B.C. see **have V.B.C.**

veg / vegetate to do nothing, to be in a trancelike state | All I wanted to do was vegetate after the grueling exam. [C455 college students: veg 'to relax luxuriously and do nothing'; U83: vegged 'intoxicated', 'daydreaming']

VEG

vein see **drain the dragon**

vicious very good, neat | My dress for the party was so vicious, all eyes were on me. [C456 teenagers: 'excellent, superb, wonderfully attractive']

victim see **fashion victim**

__ **-ville /** __ **-ville, U.S.A.** someplace where there

are a lot of (noun)'s or where a lot of (verb)-ing is done | My Astro 3 class is jockville, U.S.A. Everyone seems to be an athlete. | Sometimes you go out on the intramural field and it's just Greekville. | In my apartment it's total studyville. [C424: -ville]

V.P.L.s see **have V.P.L.s**

Vu ja dé! I have never done anything like this before! | I can't believe we are sitting in the middle of the street playing cards. Vu ja dé! [<déjà vu]

Ww

wad see **dickweed**

Wake it! Get with it!

Walk with me, talk with me! What is the matter? What is the problem? Tell me about it | My roommate looked really upset and so I said, "Walk with me, talk with me," and she started to tell me what was bothering her.

walking __ person with the knowledge of a (reference book) | walking thesaurus | walking encyclopedia | walking R.A. manual

wannabe 1. person trying to be accepted by a group, adopting its appearance and manners,

< > marks words or usages that may be offensive to some or all speakers and that therefore should be used only with discretion; C = Chapman's *New Dictionary of American Slang*; U = previously collected UCLA slang. See the Introduction for more discussion. The Pronunciation Guide provides an explanation of the symbols used in phonetic transcriptions.

poser; person who wants to achieve a goal (but who may have no apparent hope of making it). 2. would-be | She's a wannabe soc. [<wanna + be. See also **just-raped look.**]

want some / be after some to want sex [See also **get some.**]

want to front see **try to front**

wasted 1. drunk, intoxicated. 2. exhausted | Dude, I drank eight beers; I was so wasted. | I was so wasted after staying up all night, I came home from class and fell asleep. [C460 narcotics & cool talk: 'intoxicated by narcotics'; U83: 'drunk']

water buffalo to vomit | You yakked, you bisoned, you water buffaloed! [See also **bison, yak.**]

watermelons large breasts

way very, so | Derek is a great person— he is way cool. [U84, 87]

WATERMELONS

weak no good, not up to standard, *lame* | My astronomy teacher is so weak. He thought our final was on Friday, but it was supposed to be on Tuesday. | That game was really weak. We should never have lost.

weed see **dickweed**

weeder / weeder class hard class intended to reduce the number of students in a major, especially

in the sciences [<weed (out)] + [er]

Week see **Dead Week**

weenie 1. fool, *wimp*. 2. penis | I felt like such a weenie when I went to the wrong classroom. [C461]

welch out on to decline to participate in, *flake on* | I have so much studying to do before tomorrow—I think I'm going to have to welch out on the youth group meeting tonight.

WEENIE

wench slut, mean woman, *bitch* | That girl's a total wench. I said "hi" to her and she turned around to avoid me. [C462 teenagers: 'woman']

whack 1. jerk, idiot. 2. to cut (hair)

whack the tater to kick a football really hard | He can really whack the tater.

What a trip! How weird!

what is see **Yah, gal, what is?**

WHACK THE TATER

What is the deal? / What is the deal here? What on earth is going on? What's wrong with this? [See also **What's the deal?**]

What is this, Christmas? What a surprise! What a great situation! | When my ex-boyfriend called tonight, I said, "What is this, Christmas?" to my roommate.

< > marks words or usages that may be offensive to some or all speakers and that therefore should be used only with discretion; C = Chapman's *New Dictionary of American Slang*; U = previously collected UCLA slang. See the Introduction for more discussion. The Pronunciation Guide provides an explanation of the symbols used in phonetic transcriptions.

What the hell?! / <What the fuck?!> What's going on here? I can't believe this! Ugh! | My English professor just told the class that we have a ten-page paper due on Friday. What the hell!

Whatever! I don't care. That's weird. Have it your way. I don't want to argue with you. | —I know you don't like pepperoni on your pizza, but I'm really hungry for it and I'm going to order it. You can just pick it off. —Whatever.

What's the deal? What's going on? What's happening? [See also **What is the deal?**]

➤ **what's the deal with** what's going on with, what is the story with, what's happening with | What's the deal with enrolling for next quarter? I don't even know when my enrollment appointment is.

WHAT'S THE DEAL?

wheels see **spin (someone's) wheels**

whip to fall asleep while sitting up | Astro 3 is so boring that I always start to whip after the first ten minutes.

➤ **whipper / whipper class** extremely boring class | Astro 3 is a whipper.

whipped in love, infatuated, submissive, wrapped around someone's little finger | He has her so whipped that she takes him out to

WHIPPED

dinner every night. [C344: pussy-whipped 'dominated by one's wife or female lover'. See also **pussy-whipped.**]

➤ **whipped with an ugly stick** see **be beat with an ugly stick**

white phone see **talk to Ralph on the big white phone**

whiz see **cheez whiz**

Who are you? What's your problem? Shut up!

<**whore**> slut | She's slept with so many guys—what a whore. [See also **hyperdrive whore, roadwhore.**]

< **-whore**> person who spends a lot of time with (noun), person who (verb)'s a lot | partywhore | cokewhore | bookwhore | studywhore

WHORE

wicked 1. excellent, very good, delicious. 2. bad, horrible. 3. very, really | That party was wicked good. [C467 teenagers: 'excellent, wonderful'; U84: 'excellent, very good, delicious; very, very, very']

wicked loser failure, *loser* (in a temporary way—especially, person who could have avoided being a failure) | Jay played pinball in the lobby for two hours and didn't study for his midterm. What a wicked loser!

< > marks words or usages that may be offensive to some or all speakers and that therefore should be used only with discretion; C = Chapman's *New Dictionary of American Slang*; U = previously collected UCLA slang. See the Introduction for more discussion. The Pronunciation Guide provides an explanation of the symbols used in phonetic transcriptions.

wife really serious girlfriend

wig / wig out to *freak out,* to *stress,* to be hysterical, nervous, perplexed (very often used in the form **wigging**) | He wigged out when he learned that his girlfriend had cheated on him. | I was wigging over my date with Bob because I liked him so much but I wasn't sure how he felt about me. [C468 cool talk: wig 'to behave more or less hysterically'; 1950s cool talk fr musicians: wig out 'to become mentally unbalanced, lose one's sanity'; U84: wig out 'go crazy, freak out, be surprised']

wild thing see **do the deed, the wild thing**

wilma ugly girl | That ugly girl must never groom herself. She is a total wilma. [<Wilma, a character in "The Flintstones"; U83]

wimp physically, emotionally, mentally, or socially inadequate person [C468: 'ineffectual person; a soft, silly person; a weakling']
➤ **wimpy** having the characteristics of a wimp; soft, inadequate | That was a very wimpy sandwich I bought from the Coop. [C468]

window shop / go window shopping to be on the lookout for desirable members of the opposite sex | My roommate and I window shopped at the fraternity party last night. |

WINDOW SHOP

My roommate and I went window shopping at the beach this weekend.

wired high on caffeine, cocaine, or crystal methamphetamine; hyper (especially from lack of sleep); happy, excited; prepared | I'm really wired for this test. [C470]

WIRED

womp on to have sex with

woody erection | He got a woody right before his speech. [See also **sport a woody.**]

word fashionable, *cool* | That new jacket Mary bought is so word! It must have cost a lot!
➤ **Word!** Yes! *Cool!* | Word! I got an A on my midterm! | —Tom, are you going to the meeting tonight? —Word! I always go. [C473 New York City teenagers (an exclamation of agreement and appreciation)]
➤ **Word up!** What's going on?

work 1. to beat badly (in a game); to beat up. 2. to do well on. 3. to have rigorous sex with | Jon scored excellent goals all through the game—he was really working me. | Steve is such a liar. He said he worked the head cheerleader, the Playmate of the Year, and Cher. [?C473: 'to exert one's charm, power, persuasiveness . . .'; work over 'to beat . . .'; prostitutes: working girl 'prostitute']

< > marks words or usages that may be offensive to some or all speakers and that therefore should be used only with discretion; C = Chapman's *New Dictionary of American Slang;* U = previously collected UCLA slang. See the Introduction for more discussion. The Pronunciation Guide provides an explanation of the symbols used in phonetic transcriptions.

➤ **worked** tired out

working man's smile top of the crack between (a man's) buttocks visible above the top of low-slung pants [See also **Smiley.**]

WORKING MAN'S SMILE

world see **rock (someone's) world**

worried shitless very worried

worship the porcelain god / worship the porcelain goddess to vomit into the toilet | I caught him in the bathroom worshipping the porcelain god.

WORRIED SHITLESS

wrap girlfriend | Tom has had many wraps. He has never been single.
➤ **wrapped** in love, infatuated, submissive, *whipped*

wretch person who can't find someone to have sex with | You wretch!
➤ **wretched** desperate for sex | Anyone who goes to a prostitute must be wretched.

WRAP

wrinkle see **penis wrinkle**

wukka very good-looking girl or guy (pronounced [wʊ́kə]—rhymes with "cook a") | Christie Brinkley is a perfect example of a wukka.

wuss / wussy indecisive, weak, or wishy-washy person, *wimp* (pronounced [wʊ́s], [wʊ́si]—rhyme with "puss," "pussy") | Cindy, if you can't run two more miles you're a wuss. [C475 teenagers: wussy]

Xx

X see **the big X**

Xerox see **team Xerox**

Yy

Yah, gal, what is? Hello, what's up? (addressed to a female) (pronounced [yá], to rhyme with "Ma")

yak to vomit | He yakked, he bisoned, he water buffaloed. [See also **bison, water buffalo, yank.**]

YAH, GAL, WHAT IS?

yang yang nonsense, *smack* | Jake, you talk a lot of yang yang. [See also **up the ying yang.**]

yank to vomit | Dude, I drank eight beers and then I yanked. [See also **yak.**]
- ➤ **Yank on that!** Forget that! I don't want to do that! | I thought this class sounded really interesting, but it has sixteen books—yank on that!

< > marks words or usages that may be offensive to some or all speakers and that therefore should be used only with discretion; C = Chapman's *New Dictionary of American Slang;* U = previously collected UCLA slang. See the Introduction for more discussion. The Pronunciation Guide provides an explanation of the symbols used in phonetic transcriptions.

Yar! Good! Neat! *Cool!* | Yar! Dude! Check out that sweet car!

Yeah, right! / Right! I don't believe you! Forget it! *Not even!*

yeah-man boring person | We couldn't wait to get away from Mike. He's such a yeah-man.

Yes! All right! Wow! This is *awesome! Cool!*

YEAH-MAN

ying yang see **up the ying yang**

Yo! Wait! Hey! Hi! Here! (answering roll call) | Yo! Bob! I have a question for you.

yoked very muscular, *buffed, ripped* | He was so yoked I could see every one of his abdominal muscles.

you see **Fuck you! Who are you?**

yutz fool, idiot, failure | My ex-boyfriend was such a yutz!

YOKED

Zz

zero person or thing with no redeeming qualities, person with no appeal | That guy is a total zero, there's nothing good about him. [See also **take the zero.**]

zip 1. person with no redeeming qualities, person with no appeal. 2. awful, negative, bad | I had a totally zip time at the party. [C484: 'zero, nothing']

zone / zone out to daydream, stare into space, veg, be *spaced out* | He zoned so bad that he didn't even hear the teacher call his name. [C485: zoned 'intoxicated with narcotics'; U90: zone out]

Zs see **catch some Zs**

zuke to vomit (pronounced [zúk]—rhymes with "luke") | Thank God everyone managed to zuke in the bathroom!

< > marks words or usages that may be offensive to some or all speakers and that therefore should be used only with discretion; C = Chapman's *New Dictionary of American Slang;* U = previously collected UCLA slang. See the Introduction for more discussion. The Pronunciation Guide provides an explanation of the symbols used in phonetic transcriptions.

The Index

—

➤ This Index is designed to help readers locate slang synonyms and to show the relative number of slang expressions with a given meaning.

➤ The entries in the Dictionary are listed below under broad semantic headings given in standard English, with many fine distinctions of meaning ignored. For example, *bow to the porcelain god* 'to vomit into the toilet' is indexed below under **vomit, to,** while *awesome* 'outstanding' is indexed with words meaning simply **good.** Interjections (other than those meaning **Goodbye!** or **No!**) and rhetorical questions are indexed under **Interjection** and **Question.**

➤ The organization of the Index is similar to that of the Dictionary. Index headings are alphabetized according to their first word, except that **be,** infinitival **to, something** (as in a definition like 'something undesirable'), and **type of** are ignored. As in the Dictionary definitions, all verb headings include **to.** However, transitive and intransitive uses are indexed together, with a combined heading like **dance (with), to,** for instance, including both verbs meaning 'to dance' and verbs meaning 'to dance with'.

➤ Because the major Index headings are given (as far as possible) in standard English, and because of their broad meanings, some important Index headings do not appear in any of the definitions in the Dictionary. Many guides are included to aid in finding major headings: thus, if you look up **ugly** in the Index, you will find a cross-reference to the more general term **unattractive;** if you look up **jerk,** you will see a cross-reference to the more standard expression **unpleasant person;** and so on. Cross-references to main headings are also given for later words in a heading: thus, if you look up **sex,** you will find not only words meaning 'sex', but also references to other headings containing that word, such as **oral sex** or **person of indeterminate sex.**

➤ Index headings are not, then, definitions, so it is very important to check the Dictionary definition of any word you find in the Index before using or citing it. Note too that other important information, such as variant forms and offensiveness status, is not indicated in the Index.

A a

a lot   like a mojo, major time, majorly
a lot of ___-fest, major-league, mega, shit
a real   a ___ and a half
about   like
absolute / absolutely   *see* **complete / completely**
accidental   squeeze
act badly (to), to   throw attitude, throw (someone) attitude
act crazy, to   cut up, trip
act fraudulently, to   *see* **pretend**
act in a certain way, to   penny a door, penny in, salt up, space out, swoon, window shop
act inappropriately, to   trip
act like, to   pull a ___
acting in a certain style   team, team ___
action   *see* **event, foolish action**
addict   joneser
address   *see* **term of address**
aggressive   aggro (*see also* **become aggressive, sexually aggressive person**)
alcoholic beverage   doctor, nectar, precious juice (*see also* **beer, drink alcohol**)
all right   cas
all the time   24-7
amaze, to   blow away
anal sex   *see* **have anal sex**
anger, to   piss off
angry   bullshit, miffed, pissed
angry at, to get   get off on
annoyed   bitter
annoying   snotnosed
annoying person   badass, buzzkill, kook, poohead, snotnose
annoying, something   drag
annoying, to be   bug
anxious, to become   sketch out
appear homosexual, to   flame
appointment   *see* **cancel an appointment**
argue with, to   fire on, nibble at

as soon as possible   A.S.A.F.P.
Asian, half-   happa
asleep   *see* **fall asleep**
attitude   *see* **bad attitude, having a bad attitude**
attractive   adonis, bad, bodacious, fine, fly, fresh, G.Q., industrial, jeek, nasty, skanky, sporty, studly, tight, tough (*see also* **sexually attractive**)
attractive female   betty, freak mama, filet, fly girl, freak, mazehette, skank, treat
attractive male   adonis, beauhunk, freak daddy, fly guy, god, hoss, mazeh
attractive person   babe, babe magnet, oochie, P.P.D., studmuffin, wukka
attractive, something   babe magnet
attractive, to be   rage
authority, type of   fashion police

Bb

bad   badass, bunk, butter, chickenshit, dank, deadly, fucked, gnarly, harsh, heinous, hellish, killer, lame, loser, painful, phony, piece of shit, sick, sick and wrong, sketched, sucky, thrashed, to the curb, twitty, uncool, weak, wicked, zip (*see also* **like something very bad, of a bad type, person with bad breath**)
bad attitude   attitude (*see also* **having a bad attitude**)
bad experience   buzzkill, nightie, nightmare
bad joke   good dud
bad person   fuckface, M.F., scum, scumbucket
bad situation   bitch (*see also* **in a bad situation**)
bad-tasting   rancid
bad, to be   bite, reek, suck
badly   *see* **act badly, beat badly, do badly, treat badly**
bang   booyah
basketball   *see* **play basketball**
bathroom   *see* **go to the bathroom, toilet**
be   *see the word that follows* **be** *in the definition*

beat badly, to slam, spank, work
beat, to smoke
beat up, to dooie, down, jump, mess up, rock, work
become aggressive, to go aggro
beer brewhaha, brewsky, sixer, twack
behave inappropriately at a party, to party foul
bench *see* **sit on the bench**
best *see* **the best**
beverage *see* **alcoholic beverage, beer, drink**
biceps guns
big butt-kicking, honking, mondo
bisexual person combo
bizarre *see* **strange**
B.M.W. car beemer
boots, type of fuck-me boots
boring beige, bunk, cheesy
boring person yeah-man
boring sexual partner missionary man
borrow (from), to bum, cheese off, mooch, mooch off, scrounge
borrower cheeser, mooch
bossy person hell master
bother, to be in (someone's) face, be on (someone's) ass, fuck with, get in (someone's) face, give (someone) hemorrhoids, haze
bothering, to stop get off
bouffant boofed
boy *see* **male**
boyfriend beau, beauhunk, husband, spouse (*see also* **friend**)
brag, to pop off
break up with, to bail, ding, dismiss, ratfuck, sack
breasts bodacious tatas, eyes, globes, hands, mosquito bites, teats, watermelons
breath *see* **person with bad breath**
buff *see* **trivia buff**
burn, to nuke
buttocks B.A., bubblebutt, pooper (*see also* **have one's buttocks show, show one's buttocks, top of the buttocks**)

C c

California   *see* **Northern California, Southern California**
call   *see* **crank phone call**
calm   mellow
calm down   *see* **relax**
cancel an appointment (with) or a commitment (to), to   dog, flake, flake on, gel on, jake, jake on, welch out on
car   *see* **B.M.W. car**
catch in the wrong, to   nail
celebrate, to   party
chance, to take a   *see* **take a chance**
cheat, to   snake, team Xerox
cheating   team Xerox
chemistry   chemisery
chew tobacco, to   take a dip
class, type of   sleeper, weeder, whipper (*see also* **easy class**)
close   tight
clothing   *see* **criticize clothing, dressy clothes, style, unattractive item of clothing**
cocaine   blow, coke, dolomite, powder, rock, toot
coincidence   coinkidink
cold   arctic, biting, nibbling
commitment   *see* **cancel an appointment**
complain, to   bitch
complete   full-on, royal, total
completely   big time, ___-o-rama, royally, total, totally (*see also* **very**)
complicated   hairy
con   *see* **deceive**
conceited   snotnosed
conceited female   studette
conceited person   snotnose, stud, swellhead
concentrate on, to   have missile lock
condition, type of   beer goggles, coke bottle eyes
condom   lifejacket, party hat, raincoat
conformist   tight-assed
confront, to   rush
confrontational, to be   try to front

confused clueless, sketchy
confused, to be have negative clues, sketch
consideration *see* **remove from consideration**
controller *see* **remote controller**
cope, to be unable to *see* **unable to cope**
copy, to bite
course, name of a AIDS for Grades, Rocks for Jocks, Shit Lit
coward chickenshit, gimp, piece of chickenshit
crank phone call phony
crazy gone, stupid, tweaked, twisted (*see also* **act crazy**)
crazy, to become go off
critical, to be pop off
criticize clothing, to arrest, make a fashion arrest
criticize, to bag on, bail on, base on, cut up, dog on, give (someone) flack, haze, rake on, rip on, thrash on

Dd

damn fucking
dance (with), to freak, freak on, get loose, grind, shake (one's) skirt
dating, to be be married, be talking with
daydream, to space, zone
dazed spaced
deceive, to dick, dick over, fuck with, mindfuck, pull a Fletch, stroke
deeply heavily
definitely in a heartbeat
depress, to bring down, drag down, kill (someone's) buzz
depressed bummed
depressed, to be bum
desperate for sex wretched
destroy, to trash
destructive person thrasher
diarrhea *see* **have diarrhea**
difficult intense, murder
dirt *see* **filth**

dirty nappy
disappoint, to bum out, kill (someone's) buzz
disappointment dis, dog
disease *see* **venereal disease**
disgusting chud
disgusting person or thing gagger
disheveled mangled
disorganized flaky
dizzy, to feel have a buzz
do badly (on), to be raked, choke, chunk, fuck up, mess up, munch, screw up, scrub
do good (to), to do righteous, do righteous by
do nothing, to veg, zone
do quickly, to boogie
do something (to), to bust a move, do up
do strange things, to go aggro
do the impossible, to nail Jell-O to a tree
do the minimum (in), to cruise, cruise in
do, to be all over, break out with
do well (on), to ace, crank on, jam, kick ass, nail, power on, rip, score, shred, stud out, thunder, work
do wrong to, to *see* **treat badly**
doing well in like Flynn, on fire, pimping, styling
doing well, to be be golden
dollars bones
dorm *see* **person who stays in the dorm**
downfall, to be the be (someone's) ass
drained cashed
dress unattractively, to take a fashion risk (*see also* **person who dresses unattractively**)
dress well, to pimp
dressed up dolled out
dressing in a certain style team, team __
dressy clothes Monday night attire
drink alcohol, to go to the doctor, party
drink in a certain way, to hammer
drink, to bottom, chug, consume, do a beer bong, down, hammer, pound, shotgun, slam, throg (*see also* **person who drinks a lot, time to have a drink**)
drink, type of tanka (*see also* **alcoholic beverage, beer**)

drinking game, name of a Caps, Categories, Hi, Bob! Mexicali, Mr. Smith, Odd or Even, Quarters, Rochambaud, Three Man, Thumper

drinking paraphernalia beer bong

dropout burn-out

drug / drugs party favors (*see also* **cocaine, high on drugs, marijuana, start feeling a drug**)

drunk blasted, blitzed, blotto, blown, bobo, bombed, bullshit, buzzed, comatose, fried, fucked, gone, hammered, heated, hiddy, inebriated, lit, loaded, loose, lush, messed up, mindfucked, obliterated, out of control, pickled, pissed, plastered, plowed, polluted, ripped, sauced, screwed, shitfaced, shredded, slammed, slaughtered, sloshed, smashed, soaked, stoned, tanked, tattered, thrashed, toasted, torqued, trashed, tweaked, twisted, wasted (*see also* **get drunk**)

drunk, to be be in the ditch

dumb *see* **stupid**

E e

easy cake, mick

easy class mick

easy task cake

eat, to chow, chow on, grind, grub, grub on, inhale, mac, mac on, mow, pig, pig on, pork, pork on, scarf, scarf on, scoob, vacuum (*see also* **snack**)

effeminate sweet

ejaculate, to jis, spew, splooge, spooch

elegant chichi

embarrass oneself, to do oneself

embarrass, to roast

embarrassed faced

embarrassed, to be be raked

encounter *see* **sexual encounter**

endure, to suck it up

enjoy, to be into

erection boner, woody (*see also* **have an erection**)

evaluate, to   scope
event, type of ___-o-rama, orange banana, party foul
excess   *see*   to excess
excessively, to ___   have ___-orexia
excite, to   pump, spin (someone's) wheels
excited   fired up, jacked, jaked, jazzed, psyched, stoked, wired
excited (by), to be   fire up, flip, get off on, have a C.B.
exert oneself (on), to   go balls out, go balls out on
exhausted   *see* **tired**
experience   *see* **bad experience**
expose one's genitals, to   do a fruit salad
extreme   major, mega
eye mucus   eye boogers

F f

fail (on), to   biff, bomb, brick, flag, flail
failure   brick (*see also* **unsuccessful person**)
fake a response, to   bullshit
fake tan   fake-bake
fall asleep, to   whip
fall, to   spill
farce   mockery
fart, to   crack a fart, fluff, let one go, let one rip, toot
fart, type of   barking spiders, blotcher
fast   *see* **go fast, leave fast**
fat   cheesy
fat around the waist   handles, Special K pinches
fat female   heifer, hellpig, judy
fat person   porker
fecal matter   dingleberry
feel humiliated, to   feel moldy
feel ill or lethargic, to   be dragging
feeling a drug   *see* **start feeling a drug**
feeling, type of   senioritis
feet   *see* **smelly feet**
female   bitch, chick, ho

female, type of bowhead, brickhouse, demon from hell, fag hag, freak mama, Miss __, Ms. __, nun, pirate's dream, P.M.S. monster, __ queen, sleestak (*see also* **attractive female, fat female, girlfriend, homosexual female, old female, promiscuous female, short female, sorority member, stupid female, stylish female, successful female, tall female, tease, unattractive female, unpleasant female**)

fight (with), to be in (someone's) face, throw down

filth mung, shower scum, slime

finals *see* **week before finals**

finished hist

fire, to nix

first experience, to give a devirginize, pop

first sexual partner, to be a devirginize

flatterer buttlick

flighty ditzy

flirt (with), to creep, make mac with, scam, scam on, toss

flirtatious look / looks fuck-me eyes, the fuck eye

food grinds, grub (*see also* **drink, snack,** *and names of specific foods*)

fool *see* **stupid person**

fool around, to dork off, jerk off, putz around, screw around, spank

foolish action buffoonery

football *see* **hit a football**

forget, to scrub

forgetful C.R.S.

former girlfriend old battle-ax

fraternity member frat dick, frat rat, lowlife (*see also* **member of a sorority or fraternity**)

fraternity row the Row

fraudulently, to act *see* **act fraudulently**

freshman scrub

friend/friends homeboy, homegirl, homie, posse (*see also* **boyfriend, girlfriend**)

frigid tight-assed

front *see* **get in front**

frozen yogurt froyo

frustrated *see* **sexually frustrated**

fun cranking

funny   class
funny person   cut-up, roll
funny, to be   crack

Gg

genitals   *see* **expose one's genitals, penis, testicles**
genuine   *see* **real**
gesture   *see* **make an obscene gesture at**
get drunk, to   get sloppy, load up
get high, to   load up
get in front, to   have cuts, take cuts
get into trouble, to   bend over
get involved, to   get loose
get nervous, to   shit, stress
get rid of, to   ace, blade, eighty-six
get tired, to   fade, fold
get, to   rush
get wild, to   go aggro
girl   *see* **female**
girlfriend   spouse, wife, wrap (*see also* **friend, former girlfriend**)
give a first experience to, to   devirginize, pop
give me ___   me
give (to), to   do up with, sport
gladly   so fast
go around, to   cruise
go away, to   piss off, skip on
go fast (on), to   crank on, jam, jet
go for, to   go on a ___ run
go on a search through, to   rampage
go slowly, to   truck
go, to   boogie
go to a party, to   party
go to a tanning salon, to   fake-bake, nuke oneself
go to the bathroom, to   biff, make a piss stop, make a pit stop
go to, to   go on a ___ run
go weird, to   tweak

good awesome, badass, bitchin, boss, butt-kicking, cherry, choice, classic, cool, dank, deadly, decent, def, dyno, fly, fresh, gnarly, groovy, happening, hip, hot, hype, intense, jamming, key, killer, koshe, live, nectar, nifty, orgasmic, primo, rad, raging, raw, rough, rude, solid, stellar, sweet, taste, T.F.A., trick, vicious, wicked (*see also* **do good, have a good time at a party, in a good situation, look very good, looking good**)

good person butt-kicker

good song jam

good thing butt-kicker

good looking *see* **attractive**

Goodbye! Bust a move! Chow! Hasta! Hasta la pasta! Hist! Later! Take it easy!

goof off *see* **fool around**

gullible person airhead, believer, biscuit

H h

hair, type of big hair (*see also* **person with unusual hair, pubic hair**)

hairstyle do, piece

half-Asian happa

handle (pressure), to handle, hang, hang with

happy jacked, jaked, jazzed, stoked, wired

happy person happy camper

happy, to be be in there, fire up, orgasm

harass, to roust

hard *see* **have a hard time, study hard**

hard on, to be harsh on

have a good time at a party, to party hearty

have a hard time, to die

have a one-night stand, to gig

have a poor social life, to have no life

have a wild time, to rage

have an erection, to sport a woody

have an idea, to have a clue

have anal sex with, to   bufu, ream
have diarrhea, to   have the shits
have had no sex recently, to   to be in a drought, have cobwebs
have homosexual sex with   pack
have intercourse   *see* **have sex**
have left, to   be out of there
have one's buttocks show, to   have V.B.C.
have one's panty line show, to   have V.P.Ls
have one's underwear hiked up, to   have a melvin
have oral sex (with), to   blow, give (someone) a perm, play the skin flute, talk to the mike
have poor priorities, to   have no life
have sex (with), to   ball, be laying pipe, be up to no good, beat (someone) with an ugly stick, blow, boff, boink, bone, boost, bump, bump fuzz, do, do the deed, do the deadly deed, dork, gash, get a piece of, get busy, get sloppy, get some, get some trim, get together, grind, hound, jab, jock, juice, juke, jump, jump on (someone's) bones, knock boots with, make (someone) scream, mount, nail, pile, play hide the salami, plug, poke, pump, ride the hobby horse, rock (someone's) world, romp, slam, slip (someone) the hot beef injection, square (someone's) circle, stick, throw the dagger, thump, womp on, work (*see also* **have a one-night stand, have anal sex with, have homosexual sex with, have oral sex with**)
having a bad attitude   dusty
having a menstrual period   on the rag
heavy metal music   *see* **person who likes heavy metal music**
hell   *see* **the hell**
heterosexual person   breeder
hickey   lovebite, monkey bite
high on drugs   amped, baked, blown, fucked, lit, messed up, pinned, spaced, stoned, wired (*see also* **get high**)
hippie   deadhead
hit, to   bip, dooie, get loose, get loose on, pop, stick
home   the crib
homosexual   flaming (*see also* **appear homosexual, have homosexual sex with**)
homosexual female   carpet muncher, dagger, fuzz bumper
homosexual male   bufu, butt pirate, buttboy, fembo, flamer, packer, queen, rumpranger, tail gunner

honest real
horny hungry
humiliate, to dust, mold, rake on
humiliated dusted, molded (*see also* **feel humiliated**)
humiliated, to be come out moldy
hung over hung
hungry, to be have the munchies
hurry, to haul ass (*see also* **go fast**)
hurt, to tweak
hyper spazzy, wired
hyper person spaz
hysterical, to be wig

I i

idea *see* **have an idea**
idiot *see* **stupid person**
ignorant clueless
ignore, to blow off, dis, dog, gaff
ill *see* **feel ill**
illegal U-turn *see* **make an illegal U-turn**
immature person seventh grader
important key
important person or thing the shit
impossible *see* **do the impossible**
impregnate, to pop
impress, to try to *see* **person who tries to impress, try to impress**
in a bad situation popped, S.O.L., up shit creek
in a bad situation, to be be hating life, be history, be illin
in a good situation, to be be loving life
in a place, to be hang, kick it
in front of *see* **get in front**
in love *see* **infatuated**
in the way, to be be hanging big bootie out
in trouble fucked, screwed, stewed (*see also* **get into trouble**)
in trouble, to be be dust, be history

inadequate   wimpy (*see also* **weak person**)
inappropriately   *see* **behave inappropriately at a party**
indeterminate sex   *see* **person of indeterminate sex**
individualistic   artsy
inexperienced person   *see* **weak person**
infatuated   pussy whipped, whipped, wrapped
influx of __   invasion
instigate something, to   throw down
insult   dis, burn, burn on, face, rag
insult, to   burn, cap, cap on, dust, gaff, get off on, gouge, haze
insulted   dusted
intelligent student   smack
intense, to be   go off
intercourse   *see* **have sex, sex**
interesting   trick
interjection   Bag that! Balls out! Be real! Bend over! Betty rub!
B.F.D.! Big shit! Bite me! Bonus! Brainfart! Bump that! Burn!
Bust! Buzzkill! Can you say "__"? Carpe diem! Check it out!
Cheez whiz! Clue in! Come on! Dude! Dude man! Easy! Eat
me! F! Face! False! Fear! F.O.! Fuck a duck! Fuck me! Fuck
me hard! Fuck that noise! Fuck you! Fucking A! Get a job! Get
a life! Get out of here! Get out of my face! Good deal! Good
future! Gouge! Hang a bootie! Have some __! Hello! Hell's
bells! Hobbes! Hold the phone! How rudeness! Intense! Isn't
that special! Later! Let's vamos! Lick me! Lick my love pump!
Location joke! McFly! Mouth-O! Multiple sadness! Nasal on
that! No biggie! No bitch! No doubt! No shit! No shit, Sherlock!
No way! No wire hangers! Not! Not even! Party! Piss off!
Psych! Pull a clue out of the clue bag! Rock out! __'s balls are
hot! Scheize! Score! See ya! Shacks! Sheesh! Shine! Shit happens! Shitlaw! Shock a broe! Shotgun! Shut up! Sob! Stoke
me! Suck! Surf or die! Swoon! Swoop! Take a Midol! Take a
picture! Take it down a thousand! Take it easy! Take it on!
That's cool! That's quacked! __ this! Totally! Vu ja dé! Wake
it! Walk with me, talk with me! What a trip! What is this,
Christmas? What the hell?! Whatever! Who are you? Word!
Word up! Yah, gal, what is? Yank on that! Yar! Yeah, right!
Yes! Yo! (*see also* **Goodbye! No!**)
intoxicated   *see* **drunk**
involved   *see* **get involved**

Jj

jerk *see* **unpleasant person**
joke *see* **bad joke, play a practical joke on**
just like

Kk

kick a football, to whack the tater
kidnap, to bag
kidnapping bag
kiss, to mash, mash with, play tonsil hockey
knowledge *see* **talk without knowledge, write without knowledge**

Ll

lack of sex bootie drought
laugh, to bust up, roll (*see also* **make laugh**)
lazy person couch potato, house plant, lump, maggot, sloth
lazy, to be lump
lead on, to dog on
leave fast, to bolt, book, buzz
leave, to bail, bust a move, cruise, gig, motor
leaving *see* **on the point of leaving**
lecherous male Chester Molester, troll
left *see* **have left**
let into a line, to give (someone) cuts
lethargic *see* **feel ill**
lie to, to dog
life *see* **have a poor social life**
like something very bad like five miles of bad road
like, to be sprung on, dig (*see also* **person who likes heavy metal
music**)

line   *see* **let into a line, pick-up line**
liquor   *see* **alcoholic beverage**
list of unpleasant people   shitlist
live it up, to   suck it up
look unattractive in, to   take a fashion risk with
look, type of   last call look (*see also* **flirtatious look**)
look very good, to   bust fresh
looking for, to be   be on a mission
looking good   sporting, styling
looking a certain way   gothic
lose one's temper, to   go off
lose, to   be raked
lot   *see* **a lot**

M m

major subject   scene
major, type of   flake major
make a mistake   *see* **do badly**
make a pass at, to   come on to, hit on, jump, rush, scoop on, swoop on
make a target, to   have missile lock
make an illegal U-turn, to   flip a bitch
make an obscene gesture at, to   give (someone) the bird, flip off
make laugh, to   bust up, crack, cut up, roll
make out (with), to   cook up with, creep, get some, get some scrumptious, get together, grab, grab on, grovel, mash, mash with, maul, scam
make, to   bust
male   scully
male misfit   guy
male, type of   Joe __, __ king, Mr. __, N.G.B., Random Joe, Smiley (*see also* **attractive male, boyfriend, fraternity member, homosexual male, lecherous male, nice male, promiscuous male, unattractive male**)
man   *see* **male**
manly   industrial

many   *see* **a lot**

marijuana   bud, buds, doobage, doobie, ganja, geeba, Mary Jane, M.J., primo (*see also* **smoke marijuana**)

masturbate, to   jack off, play the skin flute, spank, stroke

mean   arctic, messed up, tight (*see also* **say something mean**)

mean person   asshole, bitch

mean (to), to be   dick, dis

member of a sorority or fraternity   Geek, Greek (*see also* **fraternity member, sorority member**)

membership   *see* **refuse membership**

menstrual period   Aunt Flo, monthly bill, the big X (*see also* **having a menstrual period**)

mess up, to   munch

messed up   *see* **in trouble**

meticulous person   Sally, Bonnie Brillo

microwave oven   nuker

microwave, to   microblast, nuke

middle seat   bitch

minimum   *see* **do the minimum**

misfit   barney, beau, cadet, dode, doofus, duck, dumbfuck, eggo, fred, geek, gork, mutant, nerd, squid (*see also* **male misfit, unsuccessful person**)

mistake, make a   *see* **do badly**

money   *see* **dollars, out of money**

mucus   *see* **eye mucus**

muscular   buff, cut, ripped, tight, yoked

music   *see* **person who likes heavy metal music**

Nn

nag, to   rag on, rip on

naive person   hick

natural-looking   crunchy

negative   *see* **No! not at all, nothing, receive negative feedback, say negative things, talk in a negative way**

nervous   *see* **get nervous**

nice male   SNAG

night   *see* **stay up all night**
No!   N! Nasal! Not! Shine!
nonsense   B.S., bullshit, smack, yang yang (*see also* **talk nonsense**)
Northern California   No Cool
nosy about, to be   be in (someone's) crack
nosy person   lookie-lou
not at all   not even
not to be stupid   get a clue
not understand, to   fail
nothing   jack

O o

obnoxious   obno, obnoc
obnoxious person   fuck-up
obscene   *see* **make an obscene gesture at**
obvious / obviously   ob
of a bad type   from hell
offer   *see* **refuse an offer**
old female   biddy
old person   bluehaired, grayhaired
on the point of leaving, to be   be out of here
one-night stand   *see* **have a one-night stand**
opposite sex   *see* **person of the opposite sex**
oral sex   knobber (*see also* **have oral sex with**)
ordinary   random
ordinary person   random person
out of it   mc^2, nerdy
out of money   cashed
out of place, something   snack
out of touch with reality   spacy
outcast   *see* **misfit**
outdated   cheesy, cheez whiz
outsider   random person
oven   *see* **microwave oven**
overreacting   out of control

overrun with sorority members   sorrow
overweight   *see* fat

Pp

painful testicles   blue balls
paint   *see* scratch the paint off
panty   *see* have one's panty line show
paper, type of   McPaper
paranoid, to be   sketch out
parents   Ps
park one's car in a certain way, to   be hanging big bootie out
partially smart   book smart
partner   *see* boring sexual partner, first sexual partner
party   *see* behave inappropriately at a party, go to a party
party, type of   kegger, rager, thrasher
pass   *see* make a pass at
pass gas   *see* fart
pass, to   swoop on
penis   burrito, dragon, lovesteak, ralph, rod, snake, third leg, trouser trout, tubesteak of love, weenie
people   cast of characters
perfect, to be   be golden
period   *see* menstrual period
person   dude, scully
person of indeterminate sex   dunt
person of the opposite sex   M.O.S.
person, type of   art fag, B.A.V., beastmaster, Bonnie Brillo, bubblebutt, budman, bum, Cap'n Toke, couch commander, C.S.P., Cujo, deadhead, dog, donor, fashion criminal, fossil, fuck-up, G.D.I., ghost, goob, gothic, granola, hairball, hang, hick, leech, lightweight, Magoo, ___-meister, mindfuck, monkey, ___-monster, mooch, ___-oholic, pizza face, puderhead, rager, random person, scammer, sleazebag, soc, thumber, tight-ass, trendoid, vacuum, walking ___, wannabe, ___-whore, wretch (*see also* annoying person, attractive person, bad person, bisexual person, boring person, bossy person, female, freshman, friend, funny person, conceited person, coward,

destructive person, gullible person, half-Asian, happy person, heterosexual person, hyper person, immature person, important person, intelligent student, lazy person, male, mean person, misfit, nosy person, old person, ordinary person, phony person, popular person, promiscuous person, sexually aggressive person, skateboarder, strange person, strong person, studious person, stupid person, successful person, superficial person, tired person, unpleasant person, unsuccessful person, useless person, weak person, wild person)

person under stress   stress case, stressmonger
person who dresses unattractively   fashion victim
person who drinks a lot   brew-hound, keg fly, lush, sponge
person who likes heavy metal music   hesher, metal head
person who stays in the dorm   dorm rat
person who tries to impress   brownnose, brownnoser, kiss-ass, sucker
person who uses drugs   stoner
person with bad breath   dragon
person with unusual hair   Brillohead, pubehead
pester, to   chew on
phone call   *see* **crank phone call**
phony   plastic
phony person   perpetrator, poser, pseudo-___
photographer   photog
pick-up line   rap
place, type of   Babylon, B.F.E., Bumblefuck, ___ hang, Hell's Bells, ___-ville (*see also* **in a place**)
plan   scene
plan to be at, to   be there
play a practical joke on, to   ratfink
play basketball, to   shoot hoop
please, to   stoke up
pledge   lowlife
political science   party sci
poor   *see* **have a poor social life, have poor priorities**
poor value   rip
popular   cosmo
popular female   studette
popular person   stud

practical joke   *see* **play a practical joke on**
pregnant   preg
preparation   *see* **talk without preparation**
prepared   wired
pressure   *see* **handle pressure**
pretend (that), to   perpetrate, perpetrate like
pretty   dyno
produce, to   break out with
profound   heavy
promiscuous   hot, skaggy
promiscuous female   beddy, freak, hank, hose, hyperdrive
   whore, roadwhore, skag, skanky box, skeezer, slag, slagheap,
   strawberry, trollop, wench, whore
promiscuous male   ho, Mr. Groin
promiscuous person   ho, hoser, player
protector on a toilet seat   ass gasket
provocative, to be   throw down
pubic hair   Einstein
puff of marijuana   hit
punish, to   have (someone's) ass
pursuing me, to be   be on my jock, be on my tit
put down, to   rank on
put on the spot, to   jam up

Q q

quantity of ___   -factor
question   Did you get any pieces? Do you see skid marks on my
   forehead? Don't you hate it when that happens? What is the
   deal? What's the deal? What's the deal with?
quickly   *see* **do quickly, leave fast**
quiet   mellow

Rr

real   absolute, complete, major, major-league, ___-ola, serious
reality   *see* **out of touch with reality**
really   fully, hella, majorly, ___-ola (*see also* **very**)
receive negative feedback, to   catch flack
receive, to   bust
refuse an offer, to   take the zero
refuse membership, to   ding
relax, to   bum around, chill, chill out, cold chill, cool, gel, hang out, kick back, kick it, mellow out, settle, suck it easy, take a chill pill
relaxing   kick-back
remote controller   couch commander
remove from consideration, to   nix
reprimand, to   have (someone's) ass
response   *see* **fake a response**
rid of   *see* **get rid of**
ride a motorcycle, to   scoot
ride in a certain seat, to   ride bitch, ride shotgun
ride, type of   pump
ridicule, to   rob
ridiculous   pretty, ridic
row   *see* **fraternity row, sorority row**

Ss

salon   *see* **go to a tanning salon, tanning salon**
sane   glued
say negative things, to   try to front
say something mean, to   cap
say, to   be all, be like, break out with, go (*see also* **talk**)
scare, to   freak out
scary   hairy
scold, to   fire on
scolded, to be   catch shit
scratch the paint off, to   key

scrunched up   bunged up
search   *see* **go on a search through**
seat   *see* **middle seat, ride in a certain seat**
self   ass
semen   spew, splooge, spooch
sex   penetration, the wild thing (*see also* **desperate for sex, have anal sex, have had no sex recently, have homosexual sex, have oral sex, have sex, lack of sex, oral sex, person of indeterminate sex, person of the opposite sex, uninterested in sex, want sex**)
sexual encounter   hormone fix
sexual partner   *see* **boring sexual partner, first sexual partner**
sexually aggressive person   hormone
sexually attractive   lush, nasty
sexually frustrated   fuckstrated
shoddy   squeeze
shoes   spikes
short female   broomhilda, troll
show one's buttocks, to   B.A.
sick of   burned out on
silly   *see* **stupid**
sing well, to   blow
sit on the bench, to   ride the pine
situation   scene (*see also* **bad situation, in a bad situation, in a good situation**)
situation, type of   sketch
skateboarder   grommet, skate rat, thrasher
skip, to   fan, gaff, shine
sleep, to   catch some Zs, crash
slob   scrub
slow person   truck
slowly   *see* **go slowly**
slut   *see* **promiscuous female**
smart   *see* **partially smart**
smegma   fumunda cheese
smelly feet   frito toes
smoke marijuana, to   blow jaw, smoke a bowl, take a hit
smoke, to   hit
snack   nosh
snack (on), to   nosh, nosh on

social life   *see* **have a poor social life**
soft   wimpy
something   *see the word that would follow* **something** *in a definition*
song   *see* **good song**
soon   *see* **as soon as possible**
sophisticated looking   corporate
sorority member, or female who looks like one   muffy, sorority girl, Suzy Sorority, Tina Tridelt (*see also* **member of a sorority or fraternity, overrun with sorority members**)
sorority row   the Row
sound, type of   dooie, booyah
Southern California   So Cool
sperm   spoo
stain on one's underpants   Hershey squirt
stain one's underpants, to   blotch
stand   *see* **have a one-night stand**
stand up   *see* **cancel an appointment**
stare at, to   dog
start feeling a drug, to   catch a buzz
statistics   sadistics
stay   *see* **person who stays in the dorm**
stay up all night, to   pull an all-nighter
stay with, to   hang with
steal, to   hork, snag, snake
stereo   box
stingy   tight
stood up, to get   get iced
strange   bent, bizarre, funky, gay, hairy, homosexual, kinky, obscure, psycho, queer, random, schizo, sick, sketched, sketchy, tweaked, twisted (*see also* **do strange things**)
strange person   loon, psycho, sketch, trip
strange, to be   sketch
stress, type of   P.M.S. (*see also* **person under stress**)
strong   buff, butt-kicking
strong person   studmuffin
student   *see* **intelligent student**
studious   mc^2, nerdy
studious person   nerd, smack
study hard, to   powerstudy

study, to   crack the books, grind

stuff   scheize, shit

stupid   airheaded, beat, bonehead, brain-dead, bush-league, C.R.S., ditzy, dorky, gay, lame, spacy, subhuman, twitty (*see also* **not to be stupid**)

stupid female   biff, dimbo, ditz

stupid, not to be   get a clue

stupid person   airhead, ass, asswipe, bagger, beau, bonehead, boofa, butthead, buttlick, cheese dong, doofus, dork, dork-munder, doughhead, dumbfuck, dweeb, eggo, fred, fuck, geek, gonus, McFly, mental giant, mouthbreather, nugget, putz, remo, shmuck, simp, space cadet, sped, subhuman, twit, weenie, yutz

stupid, to act   be illin

style, type of   just-raped look

stylish   hip, G.Q., jeek, sharp, trendy, word

stylish female   Heather

submissive   pussy whipped, whipped, wrapped

successful female   goddess, ___ goddess, studette

successful person   stud, studmuffin

suffix   ___-age, ___-factor, ___-fest, ___-meister, ___-monster, ___-oholic, ___-ola, ___-o-rama, ___-whore

suggestive   C.F.M.

sunburned   baked, fried

suntan, to get a   bag rays

superficial   plastic, sorority

superficial female   fifi, Heather, Tina Tridelt

superficial person   foof

surprise, to   freak out

surprised, to be   flip, freak out, lose it, shit, sketch out, spaz out, tweak, twig out, wig

sweet   *see* **think something is sweet**

sweet to, to be   give (someone) cavities

switch around among, to   play musical ___

T t

tailgate, to   be on (someone's) ass
take a chance, to   go for it
take drugs, to   party
take far away, to   bag
take (from), to   bum, gouge, mooch, mooch off, scrounge, snag
talk in a certain way, to   go off
talk in a negative way (about), to   rag on, talk head, talk shit
      (*see also* **criticize**)
talk nonsense, to   talk shit
talk without knowledge, to   B.S., bullshit
talk without preparation, to   be ticking
tall female   tree
tampon   submarine
tan   *see* **fake tan**
tanning salon   fake-bake (*see also* **go to a tanning salon**)
target   *see* **make a target**
task   *see* **easy task**
tasteless   tacky
tasting   *see* **bad-tasting**
tease   ball buster, dicktease, pricktease, trap
tease to,   roust
temper   *see* **bad attitude, lose one's temper**
term of address   babe, dude, Holmes, homeboy, homegirl, homie
testicles   nads (*see also* **painful testicles**)
the best   the kind
the best, to be   rule
the hell   the fuck
thin   pinner
thin person   pinner, twig
thing   puppy, thang
think something is sweet, to   have cavities
time   *see* **have a wild time, waste time**
time for taking pictures   Kodak moment, photo opportunity
time to have a drink   Miller time, tank time
tired   burned out, burnt, cashed, nappy, smashed, trashed,
      tweaked, tweaked out, wasted, worked (*see also* **get tired**)
tired of, to be   be over

tired person folder
tired, to be be dust, be raked
tiresome, something drag
to *see verb that follows* **to** *in a definition*
to excess off one's ass, up the butt, up the ying yang
tobacco *see* **chew tobacco**
toilet biffy (*see also* **protector on a toilet seat**)
top of the buttocks working man's smile
total / totally *see* **complete, completely**
touch *see* **out of touch with reality**
towel, type of mung rag
town *see* **place**
treat badly, to dis, dog, dupe, jerk, juke, ream, sack, screw
trendy cosmo
trivia buff "Jeopardy" champion
trouble *see* **get into trouble, in trouble**
troublesome *see* **annoying**
try to impress, to blow smoke up (someone's) ass, brownnose, kiss ass, kiss up to, suck up, suck up to (*see also* **person who tries to impress**)

Uu

ugly *see* **unattractive**
um fucking
unable to cope, to be lose it
unappealing person zero, zip
unattractive beat, buttly, coyote ugly, dorky, fugly, gay, hid, mufugly, nightmare, nisty, piss ugly, rancid, rank, raunchy, scary, scummy, skaggy, skanky, stank, to the curb (*see also* **look unattractive in**)
unattractive female broomhilda, bushbitch, bushpig, freak, hellpig, skag, skank, slag, slagheap, strumpet, troll, wilma
unattractive item of clothing fashion risk
unattractive male eddie, lou
unattractive person bagger, barney, nightie, nightmare, one bagger, prom date, scrounge, two bagger

unattractive, to be   be beat with an ugly stick, have a good personality

unattractively   *see* **dress unattractively**

unbelievable   bogus

underpants   *see* **stain on one's underpants, stain one's underpants** (*see also* **panty, underwear**)

understand, to   dig (*see also* **not understand**)

understand, to not   fail

underwear   *see* **have one's underwear hiked up, panty, underpants, yank (someone's) underwear**

undesirable, something   piece (*see also* **unpleasant**)

unfair   bogus, bush-league, fucked

unfair to, be   dick

unfortunate, something   bummer

unfriendly   on the rag, O.T.R.

unhappy, to be   be hating life, bug

uninterested in sex   asexual

uninvolved, to be   be single

university, type of   Pretty People U.

unpleasant   hid, nasty, rank, reesch (*see also* **list of unpleasant people**)

unpleasant female   hoitch, rag, skank, turbobitch, turboslut, wench

unpleasant male   buttboy, penis wrinkle, prick

unpleasant person   assface, asshole, asswipe, bagger, bub, buttlick, dick, dickhead, dickweed, dode, fuck, hemorrhoid, hoser, scum-sucking pig, shmuck, sleazebag, squid, the shake, whack

unpredictable   aggro

unreliable   flaky

unreliable person   flake

unsuccessful   lame

unsuccessful person   fuck-up, gimp, goob, gork, homo, loser, screw-up, twit, wicked loser, yutz (*see also* **misfit**)

unusual   *see* **person with unusual hair**

upset   miffed, pissed off

upset, to   drag down, piss off

upset, to be   die

urinate, to   drain the dragon, knock the dew off the lily

useless person   lump

useless, to be   lump
U-turn   *see* **make an illegal U-turn**

V v

venereal disease   oozing scabs
very   butt, butt-ass, def, fucking, hecka, mega, mondo, totally, way, wicked (*see also* **completely**)
virgin   cherry
virgin, to be a   have one's cherry
vomit   barf, technicolor yawn
vomit, to   barf, be to the curb, bison, blow, blow chunks, boag, boot, bow to the porcelain god, chew the cheese, chum the fish, chummy, chunk, drive the bus, earl, fred, hug the porcelain god, lose it, make love to the porcelain goddess, pray to the porcelain god, ralph, reverse gears, ride the Buick, spew, talk to Ralph on the big white phone, toss, toss one's cookies, water buffalo, worship the porcelain god, yak, yank, zuke

W w

wait, to   hold down
walk, to   hoof it
want sex, to   want some
want, to   jones for
waste time, to   have no life
way   *see* **in the way**
weak person   gimp, newt, wimp, wuss
wear, to   break out with, sport
week before finals, the   Dead Week
weird   *see* **go weird, strange**
well   *see* **do well, doing well, dress well**
white   pasty
wild   aggro, out of control, raging, thrasher (*see also* **get wild, have a wild time**)

wild person   animal
woman   *see* **female**
worn out   thrashed
worried   worried shitless
worry, to   shit, stress
would-be   wannabe
wreck, to   thrash
write without knowledge, to   B.S., bullshit

Y y

yank (someone's) underwear, to   give (someone) a melvin
yell at, to   blow at, get loose on
yogurt   *see* **frozen yogurt**
yummy   nummy

References

—

Aranovich, Florencia Raquel, Susan E. Becker, Gina Laura Boza-jian, Deborah S. Creighton, Lori E. Dennis, Lisa R. Ellzey, Michelle L. Futterman, Diana Geraci, Ari B. Goldstein, Sharon M. Kaye, Elaine M. Kealer, Irene Susanne Veli Lehman, Lauren Mendel-sohn, Joseph M. Mendoza, Albert C. Nicholson, Kelley Poleynard, Lorna Profant, Katherine A. Sarafian, and Lisa Michele Vander-burg. *U.C.L.A. Slang: A Dictionary of Slang Words and Expressions Used at U.C.L.A.*. Ed. By Pamela Munro. Occasional Papers in Linguistics, no. 8. Los Angeles: Department of Linguistics, UCLA, 1989.

Algeo, John. "Where Do All the New Words Come From?" *American Speech* 55 (1980): 264–77.

Chapman, Robert L. *New Dictionary of American Slang*. New York: Harper & Row, 1986.

Dumas, Bethany K., and Jonathan Lighter. "Is *Slang* a Word for Linguists?" *American Speech* 53 (1978): 5–16.

Eble, Connie C. "Slang, Productivity, and Semantic Theory." *LACUS Forum* 6 (1979): 215–27.

———. "Slang, Productivity, and Semantic Theory: A Closer Look." *LACUS Forum* 7 (1980): 270–75.

———. "Slang and Cultural Knowledge." *LACUS Forum* 12 (1985): 385–90.

———. *College Slang 101*. Georgetown, CT: Spectacle Lane Press, 1989.

———. "The Ephemerality of American College Slang." *LACUS Forum* (forthcoming).

Maurer, David W., and Ellesa Clay High. "New Words—Where Do They Come From and Where Do They Go?" *American Speech* 55 (1980): 184–94.

Munro, Pamela, ed. "UCLA Slang." Department of Linguistics, UCLA. Typescript, 1990.

Partridge, Eric. "General Considerations." Part I of *Slang To-Day and Yesterday*. 1933. Rev. ed. London: Routledge and Kegan Paul, 1970, pp. 1–36.

———. *A Dictionary of Slang and Unconventional English*. Rev. ed. by Paul Beale. London: Routledge and Kegan Paul, 1984.

Smith, Jack. "Campus-Speak." *Los Angeles Times Magazine*, 13 August 1989, p.2.

Wentworth, Harold, and Stuart Berg Flexner. *Dictionary of American Slang*. 2d supplemented ed. New York: Thomas Y. Crowell, 1975.